THE ARCHITECTURE OF ENGLAND

FROM NORMAN TIMES TO THE PRESENT DAY

By **FREDERICK GIBBERD,** F.R.I.B.A., A.M.T.P.I., A.I.A.A.

Chartered Architect. Town Planning Consultant. Registered Industrial Designer. Member of the Modern Architectural Research Group, The Design and Industries Association, etc. Joint Author of " The Modern Flat "

PREFACE

I have written this book to explain English Architecture. One sees articles in the press or hears people talking about books, wireless, golf, films, gardening, and a host of other things, but never about architecture. This is altogether deplorable, because quite apart from the fact that we spend the greater part of our time either using or looking at buildings, and quite apart from the fact that architecture is both a fine art and an exact science, the design of buildings is an activity at which the English have excelled and still do excel.

The only possible explanation for the Englishman's diffidence towards his architecture is that no one has demonstrated to him how superb and how interesting it is. There are, of course, numerous books on English architecture, but they deal, for the most part, with some specialised or technical aspect, such as building materials, the house or a similar architectural type, the lives of architects or a particular period of architecture. The books that are intended for popular consumption seldom show how the architecture has evolved from the life of the people and never extend beyond the eighteenth century. Architecture is taught in a few schools but invariably with an archæological bias. Children are taught the difference between Gothic crockets and ball flowers, rather than that the Gothic cathedral is a perfect example of the fusion of art and engineering, and is a product of a feudal society, spiritual power and a particular building material.

This book is intended to demonstrate the complete evolution of English architecture from Norman times until to-day ; to show why different building types were erected, and to explain their significance and characteristics.

There is a Chinese proverb which says " A picture is worth a thousand words." As this is so very true of a complex visual art like architecture—a picture immediately showing what would take pages to describe—I have made it, for the most part, a picture book. It is arranged so that each period occupies two facing pages. On the right-hand page are pictures of typical architectural types and on the left an explanation of these types by means of notes and diagrams. Thus by turning over the pages of the book, the evolution of English architecture from Norman to modern times unfolds itself. It must be remembered that the evolution is one continuous growth, there are no sharp breaks, and the division of architecture into definite periods is purely for the sake of convenience.

Now, architecture results from the way we behave, what we think about, and the materials we have at our disposal ; it is not a fine art separate from everyday existence. A historical note and pictures are, therefore, given at the top of each explanatory page to show the type of people who produced the buildings, their social background, and any important innovation. For example, on page 39 is a picture of St. Pancras Station which, in its time, was a new building type brought about by a new way of travelling and a new cheap building material—iron ; therefore, on the opposite page are diagrams of the blast furnace and the early railway engine, together with notes on the Industrial Revolution.

I hope that you will make a point of actually seeing the buildings illustrated in this book— a photograph can only give one view-point—and this book will help you to look at them with an added appreciation and enjoyment. You might even plan a week-end or holiday round some of them. Should you wish to do this, you will find at the bottom of each page a list of important buildings of each period under the heading " Buildings to See."

Like most authors who do not write primarily for a living—I am an architect—I have an axe to grind. It has two edges. The first is this : if you understand the evolution of English architecture you will do all in your power to encourage its further growth in the Modern movement. Should you yourself contemplate building, find out who designed the particular building you admire and write to the architect. It does not matter if you do not know him, or how brilliant or obscure he is, he will be pleased to help you. However, few of us are actually responsible for erecting a building ; but, nevertheless, by attempting to understand and appreciate good architecture, and thereby creating a greater public interest in it than at present exists, everyone can help to ensure that our new buildings are worthy successors to those of the great periods of architectural history.

The second edge to the axe is, that the more you appreciate English architecture the less it will be destroyed. There would be a public outcry if Salisbury Cathedral was demolished, but buildings which, in their own way, contribute just as much to our architectural heritage are being destroyed or defaced almost daily. Societies exist for the preservation of buildings of architectural importance, but they cannot be efficacious until the majority of the people are of the opinion that our architectural heritage is part of the cultural background of the nation, and is therefore worth keeping.

I am indebted to the generosity of the artists, authors, and publishers, whose names are given below, for permission to use their illustrations. Mr. Alan Hastings assisted with the format and typography, my brother Philip with the sociological notes, my brother Charles and Mr. B. A. Bowles with many of the drawings. Finally, I am indebted to my wife for helpful criticism and suggestions.

Frederick Gibberd.

A C K N O W L E D G E M E N T S

THE author and publishers wish to make acknowledgement to the following:

Sir Banister Fletcher, PP.R.I.B.A., F.S.A., for his permission to reproduce the drawings of the Orders (page 6) from *A History of Architecture on the Comparative Method* (B. T. Batsford, Ltd.). Messrs. B. T. Batsford, Ltd., for the drawings of the Parthenon and Pantheon (page 6) from *A Short Critical History of Architecture*, by H. H. Statham, and for the block on page 25. *The Royal Institute of British Architects Journal* for the illustration of the Pont du Gard (page 7), and the photograph of a weather clock (page 26). The Victoria and Albert Museum for the illustration of the Bayeux tapestry (page 8). Mr. Frank Risdon for the photographs of Hereford and Durham Cathedrals (page 9). The British Museum for illustrations of a knight, serf and clerk (page 10), travel in the fourteenth century (page 14), mediæval agriculture (page 16), and Lloyd's coffee house (page 28). The Executors of the late Nathaniel Lloyd, O.B.E., for the illustrations of Dover Castle (page 9), Stokesay Castle (page 21), Kirby Hall (page 21), Knole Park (page 21), Thorpe Hall (page 23), Queen Anne's Gate (page 29), and an Adam ceiling (page 30), all taken from *A History of the English House* (Architectural Press). Mr. Cyril Power for the drawing of Westminster Abbey (page 12) from *English Mediæval Architecture* (Talbot and Co.). *The Illustrated Carpenter and Builder* and Mr. Sydney E. Castle, F.R.I.B.A., for the latter's drawings of a door (page 16) and fireplace (page 20). *The Parthenon* for illustrations of King's College Chapel (page 17), St. Pancras Station (page 39), Boots Factory and Bexhill Pavilion (page 47). *Architectural Design and Construction* for the illustration of the Moot Hall, Aldeburgh (page 19), and Mr. John Hatton, Spa Director, Bath, for the photograph of the Crescent, Bath (page 31). Messrs. Shell Mex and B.P., Ltd., for illustrations (pages 25 and 33) from the *Shell Guides* to *Wiltshire* and *Devon*. Mr. B. Hackett for the water-colour of St. Philip's, Birmingham (page 29). Mr. Raymond McGrath, A.R.I.B.A., joint author of *Glass in Architecture and Decoration*, for the illustrations of a shop-front (page 31) and the Crystal Palace (page 39). Messrs. W. Flavel, Leamington, for the drawing of a kitchener (page 34). Mr. J. D. M. Harvey for drawings of small architectural details on pages 14, 18, 20 and 30. Mr. W. Scott, Bradford, for the photograph of York Minster (page 15). The London Survey Committee and the National Maritime Museum, Greenwich, for the drawing of the Queen's House, Greenwich (page 22).

4TH CENTURY B.C.-11TH CENTURY A.D.   ANTECEDENTS

Before beginning the book proper with Norman architecture it is necessary to consider the architecture of the ancient civilizations of Greece and Rome. This had, and still has, a great influence on that of England. Anglo-Saxon and Norman architecture have their roots in the temples of ancient Greece, while after the Renaissance in Italy Classic forms were brought over from that country.

Section through the Parthenon, Athens.

GREEK.

About 400 B.C., when Britain was inhabited by barbarous tribes, living in mud or timber huts, Greek civilisation was at its highest peak. The finest examples of Greek architecture were the temples they built for their numerous Gods. The most superb of them was the Parthenon, 2. This building consisted of a simple rectangular room surrounded on the outside by columns which supported beams or "lintols" upon which rested the roof timbers. There was nothing unusual about this system of construction, but what was remarkable was the architectural perfection reached with the use of their local material, marble, in two simple elements, the column and the lintol. The main concern of the Greeks was the perfection of "form"; that is, the shape of the building both inside and out, the relation of part to part, and part to the whole. In this striving for perfection they shaped each member to a definite system of proportion, and treated it with the greatest refinement of design and execution, even introducing slight curvatures of line to correct optical illusions.

Section through the Pantheon, Rome.

ROMAN.

The Romans, who absorbed Greek culture were, above all, a practical people. They accepted the Classic principle of design formulated by the Greeks and invented new designs for the columns and new decorative features. But they found that the rules of design evolved through a column and lintol construction could not be applied to all the different building types that they required and, in consequence, they took liberties with them until the use of columns and lintols eventually degenerated into a mere decorative device. The Romans made their contribution to architecture with the arch and the vault. Their skill as engineers and the cheap labour at their disposal enabled them to form such enormous structures as their aqueducts, 4, amphitheatres, 3, and public baths.

Early Christian Basilica.

EARLY CHRISTIAN.

In 313 A.D., when Christianity was formally recognized as the religion of the Roman Empire, the Christians were no longer compelled to worship in catacombs and private homes, and commenced to build churches. The first of these were adaptations of the existing Roman Halls of Justice or "Basilicas," which were exactly suited to the purpose of Christian worship and ritual. These Basilicas consisted of a large and lofty hall or nave with side aisles, and an "apse" at one end; in this the altar was placed. A raised Judge's seat in the centre of the "apse" became the Bishop's throne. In order to keep the hall light and open the nave wall was supported on columns, and was pierced by windows above the aisle roofs, called a "clearstory." As church ritual became more complex a transept and raised choir were added.

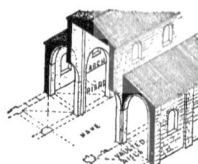

Romanesque Church.

ROMANESQUE.

In early churches the columns supporting the nave were taken from existing Roman temples, and when these were used up stone piers were built and arches and semi-circular vaults (page 8) were thrown from one pier to another instead of lintols; the construction principle of the building changing from lintol to arch. The Christian missionaries migrated across Europe in the "Dark Ages" and their religion proved a strong influence in the restoration of that discipline and order which the Roman legions could no longer maintain. They took with them this form of church architecture which is called "Romanesque"; and due to different climates and building materials each country has its own peculiarities. That in England, introduced by the Benedictine monks in the construction of their monasteries, is called "Anglo-Saxon." Later on the Normans brought over the same type of architecture but in a more developed form, and to distinguish this from the Anglo-Saxon Romanesque it is called "Norman."

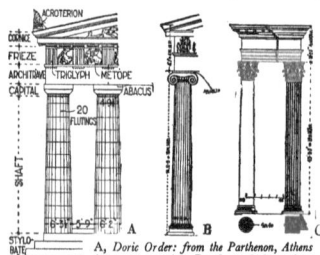

A, *Doric Order: from the Parthenon, Athens* (454-438 B.C.); B, *Ionic Order: from a Greek temple* (484 B.C.); C, *Corinthian Order: from the Pantheon, Rome* (A.D. 120-124).

THE ORDERS.

The particular types of columns invented by the Greeks and Romans, together with the lintols over them, are called the "Orders," and have had a remarkable influence on English architecture. As we shall see, they came to England via the Italians of the Renaissance (pages 20 and 22); after which English architects and archæologists studied the remains of Greek and Roman buildings at first hand and published books illustrating the Orders. Later still, those architects called the "Revivalists" even went so far as to build complete reconstructions of Greek and Roman buildings adapted for different purposes (page 36). On the left are shown the three main types of Orders, consisting of columns with their capitals and bases and the lintols above them. The bottom member of the latter is called the "architrave," the middle portion the "frieze," and the projection the "cornice." The proportions of a Classic building are based on the diameter of the column. The height of the column and of the lintol is so many times the diameter of the base. Half the diameter of the base is divided into thirty equal parts, and the height of each moulding is a certain number of these parts. Thus the proportions of all the members of the building are inter-related.

1. *Temple of Wingless Victory, Athens.* B.C. 438. 2. *The Parthenon, Athens.* B.C. 454–438.
In their chief architectural type, the temple, the Greeks perfected column and lintol construction. The columns are spaced comparatively closely together, as marble, their principal building material, will not span any great distance. The column with its lintol or beam over is called an " Order." In the illustration on the left is shown the Ionic Order, and in that on the right the Doric.

3. *The Colosseum* (A.D. 70–82), *and the Arch of Titus* (A.D. 81) *at Rome.*
The important structural development made by the Romans was the use of the vault and the arch. They built temples using the Greek post and lintol construction; but in many of their buildings they also employed the Orders as a decorative feature. In the buildings above, arched construction is shown, with the Orders applied as a decorative veneer.

4. *The Pont du Gard, Nimes.* B.C. 18.
The Romans, being essentially a practical people, brought engineering into the service of architecture. The aqueduct above, one of their greatest engineering feats, is a typical example of arched construction used to bridge a wide space.

12TH CENTURY NORMAN

1066 William I. –85 Domesday Book. –87 William II. 1100 Henry I. –35 Stephen. –54 Henry II. –59 Scutage Tax. 7–0 Murder of Becket. –89 Richard I. The Crusader. ● After the Battle of Hastings, William the Conqueror subdues the Saxons, rewarding his followers with their estates, and brings over Norman bishops and abbots to reorganize the existing Roman Catholic Church. England is therefore populated by three distinct types of society : a French aristocracy, a Latin Church under the control of the Pope, and an Anglo-Saxon working-class with their own language and customs. When the country has settled down, a peaceful invasion of French craftsmen and tradesmen takes place, and new towns grow up around the castles and abbeys. In the first part of the century the Benedictine monks have the greatest social and artistic influence, taking care of the poor and building cathedrals. Later, the Cistercian monasteries become of greater importance, particularly in the North, where they bring back to cultivation the land ravaged during the Conquest. Of the two million inhabitants quite ninety-five per cent. are engaged in agriculture. There are few towns, the most important being London, Bristol, Norwich, Lincoln, Oxford, York, Exeter, and Winchester. The countryside consists of vast tracts of forest and fen and common grazing and plough land. The majority of the people live in small villages of about 150 inhabitants, called "manors," which are run on the "feudal system." The King owns all the land and grants estates consisting of several manors to the lords provided they fight for him ; the common people, or " serfs," each hold about thirty acres of common land, in return for which they work for three or four days on the lord's land. There are, of course, different degrees of servitude, free men paying rent in kind— but generally speaking, the basis of feudal England is land, and a man's social position is judged by the amount he possesses.

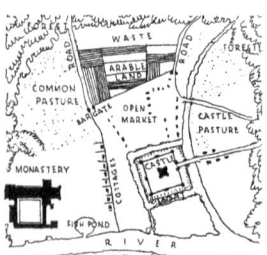

The Domesday Survey is made by William I to show the resources of the country for the purpose of taxation. It sets out the ownership of the land, the manors, mills, fish-ponds, and even the live-stock, and what it is all worth. The above sketch is based on particulars contained therein, and shows the Norman village with its castle, monastery, and huts of the serfs surrounded by the common pastures and plough land.

Part of the Bayeux tapestry in which are shown Norman warriors at the Battle of Hastings. William's easy subjugation of the country shows the need for an organized national system of defence. The feudal system meets this need ; amongst its far-reaching consequences is the division of labour, resulting in increased agricultural and military efficiency.

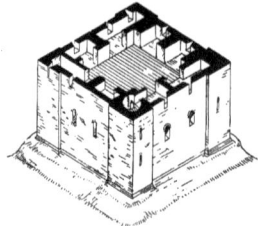

A Castle Keep. The design of the castle is based on that used in Normandy, adapted to suit local conditions. The stone tower or "keep," three or four storeys high, is the heart of the fortress, and stands in the centre of a large courtyard surrounded by a fortified wall, 5. All domestic activities take place in the Great Hall on the first and second floors, the only provision for privacy being small vaulted rooms built in the wall thickness, which serve as bedrooms. The building is draughty and comfortless, but it must be remembered that its hardy occupants are mainly engaged in fighting and hunting.

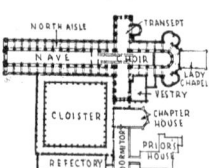

Apart from a more developed system of construction, the Norman monks bring with them the cruciform type of cathedral plan with long-aisled nave, which, due to the new environment, quickly departs from its French prototype. The plan of Norwich, above, is typical ; the comparatively close spacing of the central piers shows that the Normans cannot solve the problem of covering a wide-open space.

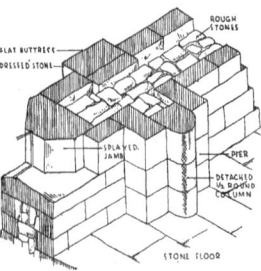

Wall and Window. The walls consist of odd-sized stones (rubble) with external and internal faces made up of carefully selected stones with smooth (dressed) faces. Where the wall is subject to an outward thrust, such as from the rib of an arch or a roof member, it is reinforced by a flat buttress. The windows are simply holes pierced through the wall, finished at the head with round stone arches. No glass is made in the country until the thirteenth century ; the weather is kept out by wood shutters or louvres, or very occasionally by imported glass.

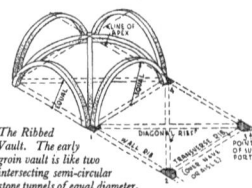

The Ribbed Vault. The early groin vault is like two intersecting semi-circular stone tunnels of equal diameter, the diagonal line of intersection being called the groin. By putting a diagonal stone rib in place of the groin, the weakest part of the vault is strengthened and less temporary wooden support is required to build the vault. Both types of vault are limited to a square plan as the wall and transverse ribs are of equal diameter.

BUILDING ACTIVITY. Norman or English Romanesque architecture (page 6) is represented by the castles built by the aristocracy as fortified homes to subjugate the Saxons, and the cathedrals and churches built by the incoming Benedictine and Cistercian monks. Considering the sparsity of the population, the achievement in the number and size of the buildings is remarkable. ● ARCHITECTURAL CHARACTER. The building material is stone, and the chief characteristic is that of mass. Walls are built of exceptional thickness and are pierced with small windows. Arches over windows, doors, and vaults are semi-circular, 6, and the supporting columns are massive and ponderous with simple "capitals," 7. Except at Durham, only small areas are vaulted (such as aisles and crypts), wide spaces being covered by wooden ceilings or vaults of a later date ; but the ponderous and massive piers and columns, 7, and the flat buttresses on the walls suggest that they were intended to be vaulted. "Details" (ornamental features) are of the simplest character, except on columns and around doors and windows, which are carved with vigorous ornament, such as the zig-zag, 7, rope, and conventional foliage. The interiors of many of the great churches are painted with figures and patterns. ● BUILDINGS TO SEE. Large portions of the following cathedrals are Norman : Durham, Ely, Gloucester, Norwich, Oxford, Peterborough and Winchester, founded and built by the monks ; Chichester, Exeter, Hereford and Rochester, served by the secular clergy. Castles: Dover, Hedingham, Rising, Rochester and the Tower of London.

5. *Dover Castle.* 1180.

6. *Arcading, Hereford Cathedral.* 1079–95. (*Window, later date.*)

7. *Columns and vault, Durham Cathedral.* 1096-1133.

The chief architectural characteristic is mass. Walls are exceptionally thick, columns massive, semi-circular vaults and arches have heavy members, and decoration is bold and vigorous, 6, 7. The home of the aristocracy is primarily a fort to withstand siege, 5.

13TH CENTURY   EARLY ENGLISH • GOTHIC

1199 John. 1215 The Great Charter. -16 Henry III. -58 The Mad Parliament. -72 Edward I. -82 Conquest of Wales. -95 Model Parliament. ● The loss of the French possessions under the indolent John severs England from the Continent. No longer merely a part of the Norman Empire, the country develops a national and distinctive character. The whole attitude of the people becomes essentially English, their buildings, customs and habits begin to express distinct national traits; and their speech, combining the French of the aristocracy, Latin of the Church, and Anglo-Saxon of the people, differs little from the English that is to be spoken seven centuries later. John is compelled by the barons, supported by public opinion, to sign the Great Charter. This is the basis of the constitutional system of future years. Written legislation incorporating traditional rights and customs takes the place of the vague expressions of the old charters. The stability and prosperity of the country owes much to Edward I., who devotes himself to the administration of Britain as a whole. To this end he conquers Wales, and attempts to bring Scotland under English rule. The foundations of a representative parliamentary system are laid when knights and citizens—representatives of the common people—attend parliament. Many of the serfs are now becoming more independent and pay rent instead of giving service. Others buy their freedom and migrate to the towns. By the middle of the thirteenth century two hundred towns have obtained the right to conduct their own affairs by purchasing charters from the aristocracy and the Church, the original owners. The friars, who come in the first part of the century, have a great moral influence on the country. Unlike the monks, the friars mix freely with the people in order to help and guide them. As they become more worldly they build up an intellectual tradition of training in mathematics, philosophy, and natural science.

A lady bathing; from a thirteenth-century illustration. The rough castles of the nobles are now being made more comfortable. Although there are no sanitary conveniences worth mentioning, the inclusion of chimneys, fireplaces and wardrobes, and the larger windows make the buildings more habitable.

A knight, serf, and clerk: from a thirteenth-century manuscript. Fighting is the career of the baron and knight, and the greatest adventures are offered by the Crusades. In their attempt to capture the Holy City, Jerusalem, from the Moslems, the Crusades are a failure, but they have a far-reaching influence. The Crusader comes back to England full of new ideas from the countries he has visited. He introduces mechanical devices, such as the clock and the windmill, new kinds of cloth and carpets, and new plants, such as the wallflower, rose tree, and lilac.

America is unknown to the medieval man; in his eyes Britain is on the edge of the world; beyond is the Atlantic ending in space. The Mediterranean is the avenue of commerce, and England, far from the main shipping routes, has few ships and little foreign trade. Right: A Crusaders' ship, A.D. 1200.

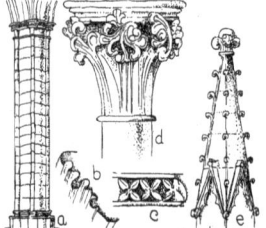

a, Pier with attached columns; b, deeply undercut mouldings; c, dog tooth ornament; d, column capital; e, pinnacle.

The introduction of the Gothic pointed arch removes the limitations of Norman vaulting. Since one arch can now be made more pointed than another, the space to be vaulted can be made rectangular instead of square. Thus, it is possible to make the nave wider than the aisles of the cathedral and the building generally more open.

Wall and Window. The wall is reduced to stone piers reinforced by buttresses. The window, stretching from pier to pier, consists of pieces of stained glass held together by lead canes between stone mullions.

GOTHIC

The word "Gothic" was invented by the Italians of the Renaissance as a term of abuse for an art they thought was the work of Goths or barbarians. The chief principle of Gothic architecture is the concentration of the weight of the building on isolated points by means of the ribbed vault, the pointed arch and the buttress.

The style grew out of English Romanesque or Norman architecture (page 6), and its development can be seen in the gradual mastery by the builder over construction in stone. As the column, vault, and pointed window develop, the style changes gradually and continuously through what are called for the sake of convenience

"Early English," "Decorated," and "Perpendicular" styles. Gothic architecture is continually attacking new problems or discovering fresh solutions for old ones; it is not the product of an individual, but the creation of ages of experience.

BUILDING ACTIVITY. The secular bishops and their canons now vie with the monks in cathedral building. Castles continue to be built, and the more peaceful conditions of the country under Edward's strong policy lead to improvements in their equipment. Additional buildings, such as the buttery, kitchen, and chapel, are erected in the castle courtyard. ● ARCHITECTURAL CHARACTER: *Gothic.* The Norman round arch, 6, and groined semi-circular vault develops into the pointed arch and the pointed ribbed vault, transforming the building into the stone-framed Gothic structure (page 12). As the window becomes larger the walls need more reinforcement, and, in consequence, the buttress becomes deeper. The massive Norman column is replaced by piers often consisting of clusters of columns. In some cases, slender columns are attached to the piers. Windows become narrow and pointed ("lancet "), and are grouped together under one arch making one wide, mullioned window, 8. Mouldings become deep chases cut into the stone, and carving is more naturalistic. Spires, steeper roofs, and parapets in place of eaves all contribute towards the development of a lighter type of building in which verticality predominates. ● BUILDINGS TO SEE. Cathedrals served by the secular clergy; York, Lincoln, Wells, and Salisbury, the most complete building in the Early English style. The Benedictine monastery, Westminster Abbey, founded in 960 A.D. Caernarvon and Conway castles, built by Edward I to keep peace in conquered Wales.

8. *The Five Sisters Window, York Minster.* 1230-40.

The round arch and vault have become pointed, making the building lighter in appearance. Narrow windows are grouped together under one large arch, 8. *With the more settled conditions of the country the house becomes less like a fort,* 9.

9. *Stokesay Castle, Shropshire.* 1240 and 1291.

12TH TO 15TH CENTURIES THE CATHEDRAL • GOTHIC

In mediæval times there is complete religious uniformity over Western Europe. The Roman Catholic Church, consisting of corporations of monks, religious orders and secular clergy with the Pope at the head, is the one Church in which all men believe. King, baron, knight, and squire, right down to the poorest serf know no good or evil outside the moral ideals of the Roman Catholic Church. It is this spiritual unity that makes possible the greatest mediæval contribution to art, the cathedral. A cathedral is not only a house of worship, but is itself a way of worshipping God. In founding and building it, patron and craftsmen are not concerned merely with making a fine building for the sake of the thing, but with the glorification of their religion. The carver of the capital or pinnacle is helping to make a house for God; his incentive is religion, not art or self-glory. The mediæval craftsman is not an artist professing any ideals other than those of his fellow men, neither is he an idealist living apart; he takes his place in society in just the same way as the butcher or the baker. Art is not an expensive hobby, a thing outside normal existence; it is a natural part of everyday existence; art and life are one, and religion makes them so.

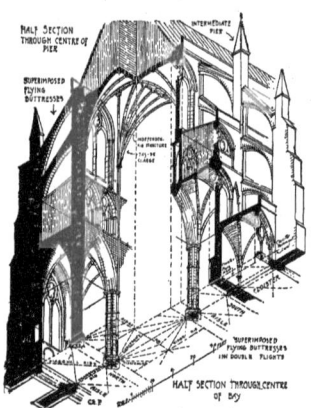

The mediæval builders do not conceive the cathedral as a work of art or an essay in design, but as a solution of the problem of enclosing a space for worship. Stone and glass are the materials at their disposal, and with them they evolve a system of building in which there is a complete fusion of art and science. Each rib, column, buttress, pinnacle, and gargoyle serves some practical and structural need, and, being for the glorification of God, is made as perfect as possible. The details of the building are worked out by each craftsman according to his fancy, the traditions of his craft, and the practical problem in front of him. The diagram above shows one bay of a cathedral (Westminster Abbey), with the vaulting ribs springing from isolated points (the piers). The flying buttresses, above the aisle roofs, counteract the outward thrust of the nave vaulting ribs.

 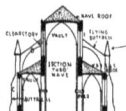  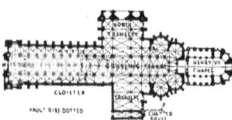 

A, Vaulting ribs.   B Decorated pier.   C, D, Buttresses.   E, Pinnacle.   F, Perpendicular window.   G, Plan of Westminster Abbey.   H, Decoration.

ARCHITECTURAL CHARACTER: *Gothic.* The chief characteristics of cathedral architecture are the ribbed vault, the pointed arch, the pier, and the buttress. By means of these the mediæval builders make a stone cage in which there is perfect structural equilibrium. The ribs direct the thrust of the vault towards definite points, where it is counteracted by thrusts from other ribs and the buttresses. The weight of the building is concentrated on isolated points, and the wall, serving no structural purpose, becomes a thin tracery of stone filled in with glass. The Vault, A, consists of slender stone ribs; the triangular spaces between are filled in with thin stone slabs. These ribs spring from the wall piers between the windows and from the isolated piers inside the building, B, which separate the nave from the aisles. The outward thrust of the vault ribs is counteracted by buttresses bracing the piers between the aisle windows, C, or by flying buttresses which brace the piers between the clearstory windows, D. The pinnacles, E, serve to weigh down the buttresses. The spaces between the wall piers are filled in with stained glass held in light stone mullions and tracery, F. ● Although the plans of most cathedrals appear to be complicated they are basically quite simple. The plan is based on a Latin cross, and is called " cruciform," G. The main body of the church, the nave, is contained in the long arm of the cross, which is directed towards the West, while the choir and sanctuary are situated on the East. The short arms of the cross form the North and South transepts. The " crossing," junction of the arms of the cross, is usually emphasised externally by a tower (Exeter, page 15), often tapering into a spire. There are often secondary towers on the West end marking the main entrance (Lincoln, opposite). ● BUILDINGS TO SEE. A list of cathedrals will be found under each architectural period (pages 8, 10, 14 and 16).

12

10. *Opposite page: Lincoln Cathedral. Rebuilt 1185-1200.*

14TH CENTURY   DECORATED • GOTHIC

1307 Edward II. -27 Edward III. -38 Beginning of Hundred Years' War with France. -49 Black Death. Statute of Labourers. -77 Richard II. -99 Henry IV. ● The peaceful conditions and prosperity which had resulted from the strong policy of Edward I are terminated by the Black Death, which kills about a third of the population, and the Hundred Years' War with France. The latter comes about through the claim of Edward III to the French throne, France's intervention in Scotland and her attempt to control the cloth-producing towns of Flanders, England's chief importers. These two calamities lead to a scarcity of labour and a rise in prices. The landlord is hit, as he still receives the same rent in lieu of service from the serfs, but has to pay higher wages for labour. Several expedients are tried, such as restoring the old rate of wages, and a return to service by labour, but all fail, and there is great discontent. As a result, many landowners lease their land for a rent and others turn from arable to sheep farming, which requires fewer men. The serfs as a class gradually disappear and feudalism begins to decline. A social change is taking place in the towns. The wealthy members have formed Merchant Guilds to protect their rights; and as they jealously guard their membership the poorer people, the craftsmen, artisans, and new settlers from the country, are forced into forming Craft Guilds for their own protection. Students are beginning to flock to Oxford and Cambridge to study under the different teachers.

Chivalry and Heraldry. The cult of chivalry directs the life of the baron and knight. Their career is fighting, and whether on the field of battle or in the tourney they observe a standard of ceremonies that is almost a religion. Heraldry records the knight's pride of birth and serves the practical purpose of being a distinctive token on the field of battle; a leader with closed helmet cannot otherwise be recognized. This pomp and splendour even affects the Church, and distinctive badges and insignia are carved on the tombs of both bishop and knight and become a decorative element, 13.

Passengers travel by horseback and goods by packhorse or crude horse-drawn carts. The Roman roads are neglected, and the few new roads are little more than rough tracks making communications difficult.

Sheep Farming. Wool is the chief industry, but it is only woven into coarse homespun, most of it being exported to the industrial towns of Flanders, where it is made into fine cloth. Some of the first examples of industrial architecture can be seen in the old wool-cleaning towers in various parts of the country.

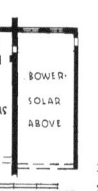

The Medieval House   The manor house, fortified by moat or wall, has now superseded the castle and become the home of the aristocracy. Manners and habits of the time are crude, and there is little or no privacy, the whole of the household living together, practically in one room. This room, the hall, is the important element of the plan. It is two storeys high, and at one end there is a dais at which the lord and his family sit at meals overlooking their retainers. Beyond this and on the second floor is the solar, their bed-sitting room. The hall is also used for entertainments, and as a bedroom for the retainers.

The hall of the manor house has an open timber roof, and, as the fire is usually in the centre of the room, an opening with louvres lets the smoke out. Walls are covered with plaster, wood boarding, cloth, and tapestries. The floors are described some years later by Erasmus as being " commonly of clay strewed with rushes, under which lies unmolested an ancient collection of beer, grease, fragments, bones, spittle. . . . and everything that is nasty." The cottages of the people (above) are mostly single-storey one- or two-room buildings constructed of mud and wattle, wood or stone, with thatch roofs and tiny unglazed windows.

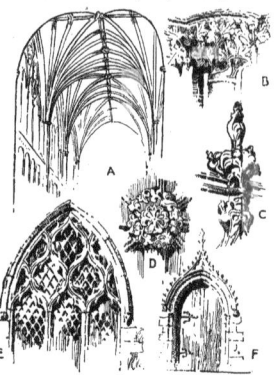

Details of the Decorated style are lavish and highly ornate. A, Vaulting, showing the ribs that carry the weight down to the wall. B, C, Naturalistic leaf ornament. D, " Boss," covering junction of vault ribs. E, Window with decorative tracery. F, Doorway with hood in the reverse curve or " ogee " shape.

BUILDING ACTIVITY. The prosperity of the country manifests itself not only in the cathedrals and abbeys, but in the building and embellishment of parish churches. Due to the Black Death, the building activity declines from the middle of the century. ● ARCHITECTURAL CHARACTER: *Gothic.* The extravagance and ostentation of the aristocracy in the first half of the century—a reaction from the severity under Edward I—is reflected in the architecture, which becomes highly ornate, and gives the name " Decorated " to the style. The gradual mastery of the mason over stone construction allows the structural members to become thinner and placed further apart, so that the building is lighter and more spacious. Geometric designs are abandoned for a more naturalistic treatment; the flowing tracery of windows branching and interweaving in a highly naturalistic but, nevertheless, still structural manner, 12. Vaulting is developed by connecting the major weight carrying ribs by minor ones called " liernes," 12, giving it a more complicated surface and allowing the members of the stone skeleton to be lighter. A new decorative element, the " ogee " or reversed curve, is used for the tracery of windows and for hoods over doorways. Carving is lavish and naturalistic; forms such as sprays of oak, vine, or maple are used to decorate the capitals of columns and piers and the finials of buttresses. ● BUILDINGS TO SEE. The following cathedrals: Exeter, the most complete building in the Decorated style; York, the great West Window; Lichfield, the arcaded and canopied front and the choir; Lincoln, the Angel Choir, transitional between Early English and Decorated; Bristol, choir; Wells, Chapter House, choir and polygonal Lady Chapel; Worcester, nave; Ely, the great central octagon—a new planning development. Parish churches in all parts.

11. *Exeter Cathedral.* 1112–1399.

12. *West Window, York Minster.* 1261–1324.

13. *Penshurst Place, Kent.* 1341.

14. *Sutton Church, Cambridgeshire.* 14th Century.

Gothic architecture is not a way of designing cathedrals but a constructional method evolved by mediæval man for all building types, 12, 13, 14. Evidence of the slow evolution of the style can be seen in most cathedrals. (Exeter, 11, is mainly in the Decorated style, but the central towers are Norman and the large east window Perpendicular.) The windows are now large expanses of glass divided up by stone mullions and highly " decorative " tracery, 12.

15TH CENTURY   PERPENDICULAR • GOTHIC

1413 Henry V. -20 Treaty of Troyes. -22 Henry VI. -51 Final loss of France. -55 Beginning of the Wars of Roses. -61 Edward IV. -74 Caxton introduces printing. -83 Edward V, Richard III. -85 Henry VII. -92 Columbus discovers America. ● Inspired and united by Joan of Arc, the French bring the Hundred Years' War and England's ambitions in France to an end. The barons with their armed retainers, which constitute the fighting force, return home. Powerful and ambitious nobles, such as Warwick the Kingmaker, each with his own private army and with no common objective, take the law into their own hands and struggle for individual power. The disputed succession to the throne between the Houses of York and Lancaster is sufficient to bring about a civil war, which is conspicuous for lawlessness and treachery. It lasts thirty years, during which most of the nobility are killed. Finally, Henry Tudor, a Lancastrian, wins the Crown and unites the Red and White Rose by marrying Elizabeth of York. Henry crushes what little power remains in the hands of the barons by disbanding their followers; and realizing the power of wealth be amasses a large fortune. The destruction of the nobility gives power to the middle classes, who have steadily become wealthier. Caring little for the rights of either side and being determined that such butchery shall not happen again, they do all they can to make the Crown so powerful that no individual can oppose it. The rise of the middle classes, development in commerce, and new inventions, tend to make the country more democratic in spirit. Money comes into general use and becomes a criterion of social standing. The invention of printing multiplies the production of books, and knowledge begins to spread.

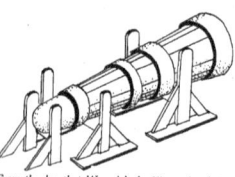

From the day that Warwick the Kingmaker batters in the doors of a castle with a cannon, the fortified home is an anachronism. But battlement coping and gatehouse are retained as decorative features.

Mediæval Agriculture. The cultivation of land is on the three-course system—the fields being sown with corn for two years and then left fallow to recuberate their fertility. This wasteful system, together with such primitive farming methods as reaping with sickles and threshing with flails, makes the production of wheat, and therefore the standard of living, low.

Power. Wind and water provide the power for grinding corn in the mills. The post mill shown above, first built in the twelfth century, continues in use until the industrial revolution.

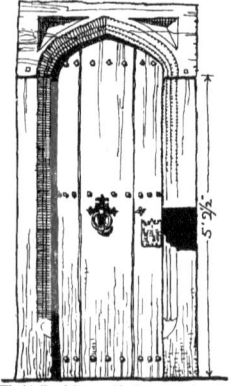

The Mediæval Door. Planks are placed vertically side by side and fixed to horizontal battens by iron studs. This rigid fixing causes the boards to split, as it is the natural quality of wood to shrink and swell.

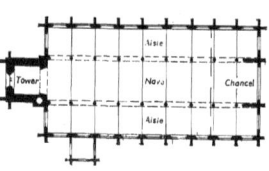

Typical Parish Church Plan. A village, not having the collective resources of the monastery, builds in an altogether smaller and more intimate manner. The structural principle and the elements are the same as those of the cathedral and show the same evolution through the centuries, excepting that in place of the stone vault is an open timber roof with trusses to carry the weight down to the buttresses.

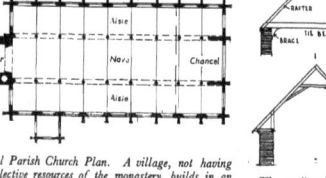

The mediæval builder prefers to cover his buildings with stone—the most fireproof material at his disposal. But as the cost of stone vaulting is enormous there grows up a tradition of wood roof construction which becomes one of the most distinctive features of English architecture. The early tie beam roof type, 1, to which is added king post and side struts, 2, is rivalled by the trussed rafter, 3, in which the rafters rest on the outside of the wall and are supported by vertical struts on the inside. Both are outshone by the hammer beam, 4, and facing page, developed from the trussed rafter by adding a bracket and further vertical support.

BUILDING ACTIVITY. The gain in wealth of the middle classes and the decline of the Church as a social and political force changes the building activity from vast cathedrals and abbeys to lesser buildings, such as parish churches, guild chapels, houses and collegiate buildings. ● ARCHITECTURAL CHARACTER: *Gothic.* Through the economic conditions ensuing on the Black Death the more severe Perpendicular style supersedes the Decorated. This style is the last stage in the evolution of Gothic architecture; in it stone construction is carried to its limit. Buildings are light open structures in which the wall is reduced to a row of thin piers between wide windows. The weight of the building and the outward thrust of the vault is counteracted by deeply projecting "wall" and light "flying" buttresses. The church and chapel roof reaches its structural and decorative limits in the stone lace known as "fan vaulting", 15, and in the wood hammer beam truss, 16. The roof becomes flatter, and leaves in silhouette the parapet; this, becoming more conspicuous, is pierced and panelled, 17. The mullions of the windows are carried straight up to hit the arch—the name of the style is derived from the upright lines of the window tracery—and the latter becomes flatter in curve and four-centred. The flat foliated panel is the chief decorative element, and is applied to walls, buttresses, wood screens, and even the surface of vaults. Ornament is more abstract and flat in surface. Heraldic devices and conventional designs are reiterated throughout the buildings. ● BUILDINGS TO SEE. Cathedral towers of Canterbury, Chester, Durham, Gloucester, York and Beverley. Fan vaulting at St. George's Chapel, Windsor; and Henry VII Chapel, Westminster. Parish churches throughout the country. Colleges at Oxford and Cambridge.

15. King's College Chapel, Cambridge. 1446-1515.

The rise to wealth of the middle classes makes the fifteenth century notable for its secular buildings, 15, 16, 17. The evolution of Gothic architecture reaches its final stage in the wide open space covered with light stone fan vaulting, and bounded by walls of coloured glass and thin stone members, 15.

16. Eltham Hall, Kent. 1476.

17. The Tower, Magdalen College, Oxford. 1458.

16TH CENTURY • 1500-50   TUDOR • TRANSITION

1509 Henry VIII. -17 Luther. -20 Field of the Cloth of Gold. -32 Beginning of Reformation. -39 Monasteries suppressed. The Great Bible. -47 Edward VI. -49 Church Services in English. ● The sixteenth century is one of great social advance in England. The strong Tudor monarchy frees the country from troubles at home or abroad, and consequently attention can now be directed to social and religious questions. Luther has protested against the worldliness of the Catholic Church and advocates drastic reforms. His Protestant religion is not supported in England, where there is no desire for changes in the Church Service. Englishmen, however, object to the power of the Popes, whom they regard as foreign princes having little interest in this country except as a source of income. So, when Henry VIII, largely for selfish motives, takes the title of "Supreme Head of the Church in England" he meets with little opposition. To consolidate his position he dissolves the monasteries, strongholds of the Papacy, and distributes their wealth and lands. Men thus enriched will be slow to support a return to Roman Catholicism. The times are cruel and gross; clever and cunning men make great fortunes, but many simple folk are reduced to a state of beggary. Prices rise when gold and silver are brought from the New World (the Spanish and Portuguese colonies of South America), the currency is debased; and the people suffer from the loss of the charity of the monasteries. On the other hand, through the revival of learning, individuals are beginning to be admired for their power of intellect rather than for their prowess on the field of battle or their religious devotion. The books and preaching of such enlightened thinkers as Colet, Erasmus, Fox, and More stir the medieval mind to new activity. The Universities prosper, and numerous new grammar schools are founded.

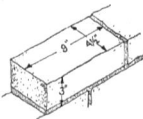

The brick is the first standardized building material. Its size, shape, and weight are such that it can be easily handled, and as long as manual building processes are used it will remain a "modern" material. Flemish refugees were making bricks in East Anglia as early as the thirteenth century, but it cannot be called a material of English architecture until Henry VIII and his Court adopt it for the construction of their mansions.

The New Patron. The dissolution of the monasteries ends the great era of church building, and the new patrons of architecture are those who share in the spoils of the monastic dissolution or profit through the widening scope for personal enterprise.

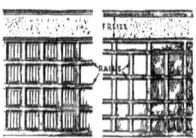

Oak panelling, occasionally used in the fifteenth century, now becomes a common form of wall finish. The panels being the width of a single plank of wood are small. The rails are wide and finished at the edge with a splay or simple moulding. The carving to the panels on the left is called "linenfold"; on the right is plain panelling of various sizes.

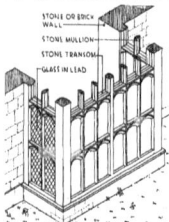

Wall and window. Weight carrying walls of stone or brick interrupted by large stone windows and bays. The opening portion of the window is constructed of iron and hinged at the sides (casement). The limitation in the size of this necessitates the comparatively close spacing of the mullions and the introduction of horizontal bars (transomes). The small rectangles thus formed are placed side by side and one above the other and form the large bays or flat windows which are a feature of sixteenth-century architecture.

The Entrance Gateway of Compton Wynyates, Warwickshire, shown above, is a typical example of the adoption of Perpendicular Gothic forms for domestic use. The low four-centred arch is enclosed within a heavy rectangular frame, and the three-light window has a square head. Over the entrance heraldry (page 14) is used as a decorative device.

In the above Tudor details the scroll is an early example of Classic detail, and the chimney is built of moulded bricks.

In Italy the Renaissance had resulted in the formation of a new architectural style based on the Classic architecture of ancient Rome. Adapted to suit the requirements of the time, the style had taken on its own distinctive features. During the sixteenth century this Italian Renaissance or Italian Classic archi-

TRANSITION

tecture has an increasing influence on that of England. Starting with a few isolated details early in the century, the style becomes more and more fashionable until buildings are decked out with Classic mouldings and columns (page 6), and the traditional irregularity of Gothic architecture is replaced by the more formal characteristics of the Classic. The continuous styles known as Tudor, Elizabethan, and Jacobean show the progressive influence of the Italian Renaissance ; the slow change from Gothic to Classic architecture. For the sake of convenience this change is called "Transition."

BUILDING ACTIVITY. The dissolution of the monasteries ends church building. Henry and his favourites employ their wealth in the building of palaces and mansions. In Edward's reign many Grammar schools are founded through the influence of the Reformation. ● ARCHITECTURAL CHARACTER : Transition. Architecture is Gothic in form, but altered and adapted for domestic use. Large mansions are built up with stone mullions and transomes, and the horizontality of the latter, together with the flattened arch, destroys the characteristic Gothic verticality. The four-centred Perpendicular arch (page 16) with a square frame is used for doors and windows, but the vault and tracery are disappearing. Houses are timber framed with panels filled in with lath and plaster, 18, or of stone construction in stone districts (page 24). Brick now becomes a fashionable material for the homes of the wealthy, 20. Battlement copings, moats, and elaborate gatehouses are retained rather as architectural features than for their original use of defence; the house is in no way a fort. The building of mansions naturally leads to improvements in design; further rooms are added; the chimney stack becomes important, 21, and more consideration is given to comfort in the interior. Ceilings begin to be plastered and painted, and walls to be panelled with wood or hung with tapestries. The Italian craftsmen employed by Henry add small ornamental features in the Classic manner, such as scrolls and plaques, and give England the first breath of Classic architecture. ● BUILDINGS TO SEE. Cowdray House, Midhurst; Hengrave Hall, Bury St. Edmunds; Layer Marney Hall, Essex; Sutton Place, Guildford; Compton Wynyates, Warwickshire; part of Hampton Court Palace; St. James's Palace.

18. *Bishop Hooper's Lodgings, Gloucester.* 16th Century.

20. *Leighs Priory, Essex.* 1536.

19. *The Moot Hall, Aldeburgh.* 16th Century.

21. *Chimneys at Hampton Court Palace.* 1520.

22. *Cringleford Bridge, Norfolk.* Early 16th Century.

The dissolution of the monasteries changes the building activity from churches to mansions. The invention of gunpowder has made defence no longer a factor in house design; but battlement copings and similar features are retained as decorative elements, 20. Although wood and stone are still the chief building materials, 18, 19, brick becomes fashionable and is exploited with great virtuosity, 21.

16TH CENTURY • 1550-1600   ELIZABETHAN • TRANSITION

1553 Mary. -55 Persecution. -58 Elizabeth. -71 Rise of Puritans. -77 Drake's voyage round the world. -88 Armada. -90 Shakespeare's early plays. -97 Bacon's Essays. ● The Renaissance, or re-birth, is the first great change in English Society after the Norman Conquest. The half-forgotten literature and art of the ancient civilisations of Greece and Rome arouse new interest; across the ocean a new world is discovered. The researches of Galileo and Copernicus revolutionize man's conception of the universe. Instead of living the small and confined life of the Middle Ages under the moral and intellectual direction of the Catholic Church, men find themselves in a world where there is unlimited opportunity for personal enterprise both in intellectual pursuits and material gain. Thus, a delight in living is created, and a joy in beauty for its own sake, whereas formerly, art and life had been in the service of the Church. The Elizabethan Church is broad enough to satisfy all but extremists, and the Act of Uniformity, compelling church attendance, is not strictly enforced. Persecution is on political rather than spiritual grounds. Elizabeth reigns ably and energetically, maintaining the balance of power in Europe and establishing peace and social order at home, and thus furthering commercial development. Furthermore, her legislature in favour of the middle classes, and for the poor, of which there are many, does much to stabilize the country and raise the standard of living. England is rapidly becoming a sea power and building up a foreign trade. The Elizabethan adventurers and the trading companies must be financed, so usury and the financier, hitherto rather despised, become respectable. Philip of Spain, the champion of Catholicism, plans an invasion of Protestant England; he is actuated also by maritime rivalry. The defeat of the Armada unites England with a burst of national enthusiasm and patriotism.

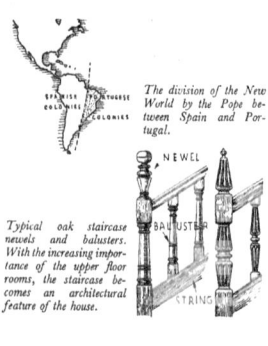

The division of the New World by the Pope between Spain and Portugal.

Typical oak staircase newels and balusters. With the increasing importance of the upper floor rooms, the staircase becomes an architectural feature of the house.

Queen Elizabeth on her way to visit Lord Hunsdon; from a painting of about 1580. In the foreground is William Shakespeare.

An Elizabethan ship. With the discovery of the New World, England is now on main sea routes. Her Merchant Adventurers cross the Atlantic; and companies are formed to trade with India, Turkey, and Russia.

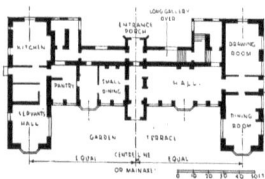

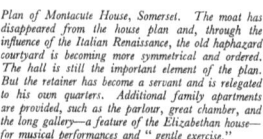

Plan of Montacute House, Somerset. The moat has disappeared from the house plan and, through the influence of the Italian Renaissance, the old haphazard courtyard is becoming more symmetrical and ordered. The hall is still the important element of the plan. But the retainer has become a servant and is relegated to his own quarters. Additional family apartments are provided, such as the parlour, great chamber, and the long gallery—a feature of the Elizabethan house—for musical performances and " gentle exercise."

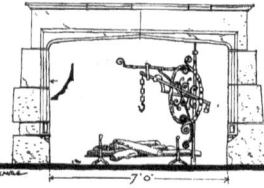

The homes of the middle classes are being made more comfortable, and many of them are re-built in brick. Glass is cheaper and comes into general use. Walls are panelled and ceilings plastered. Floors are carpeted, and pewter utensils used instead of wood. Most of the houses are in the traditional Tudor style, the Italian designs only affecting the houses of the wealthy. Above is shown an open fire with flattened Tudor arch ; the fire cradle and pot crane are of later date.

Oak carving. The ornament in the panel A is called strap work, and is also used for plaster ceilings. The mantelpiece B is a design in the Classic manner, and has Corinthian pilasters (flat attached columns); compare with the Corinthian column on page 6.

BUILDING ACTIVITY. The unrivalled opportunity for individual enterprise, and the increased wealth of the nobility and rising middle classes, make the Elizabethan period conspicuous for its domestic architecture. ● ARCHITECTURAL CHARACTER: *Transition*. The Italian Renaissance is now a definite influence on the design of large mansions. Plans are made more ordered and balanced and there is a striving for symmetry in the elevations, bay being balanced by bay, and tower by tower. Classic details are introduced in chimney stacks, doorways, and fireplaces. Windows are exceptionally large with square heads, mullions, and transomes, 24, and Gothic tracery has disappeared. But many of the houses are uninfluenced by the new fashion; of these, the half-timbered style reaches perfection, the structural wood members being exploited to form decorative patterns, 23. Interiors of the mansions are lavishly decorated with elaborate plaster ceilings and oak or plaster panelling. At the end of the century Gothic forms are fighting a losing battle against Classic; but the new details are still not properly understood and are applied as a decorative veneer with a complete disregard for Classic proportions, 25. The Transitional style is carried on far into the seventeenth century and is therefore called " Jacobean." Its character, although cruder, is essentially the same as Elizabethan; many authorities call the two styles by the name " Jacobethan." ● BUILDINGS TO SEE. Typical half-timbered houses such as Moreton Old Hall, Cheshire; the Gatehouse, Stokesay Castle, Shropshire, 23. Houses in stone which show the Classic influence, such as Montacute House, Somerset; Wollaton Hall, Nottinghamshire.

23. *Gatehouse, Stokesay Castle, Shropshire. Late 16th Century.*

24. *Kirby Hall, Northants.* 1572.

Through the influence of the Italian Renaissance there is a striving for symmetry, and Classic details such as columns and cornices are applied to the walls as a decorative veneer, 24. Interiors are finished in elaborate plaster work. The traditional wood-and-plaster type of building reaches its perfection in such buildings as the Gatehouse, Stokesay Castle, 23.

25. *The Solar, Knole Park, Sevenoaks, Kent.* 1605.

17TH CENTURY • 1600-60

1603 James I. –20 Mayflower. –22 First regular newspaper. –25 Charles I. –28 Petition of Rights. –42 Civil War. –49 Commonwealth. –53 Cromwell. • In Tudor England a strong monarchy had been necessary, at first to unite the country after the Civil War, later, for the protection of the new national religion. The Stuarts find a people respected abroad, prosperous, patriotic, and contented—conditions ideal for the growth of democracy. But wishing to rule absolutely they have no sympathy with this tendency nor with the rise of Puritanism. Owing to their Roman Catholic sympathies, they are repeatedly in conflict with the majority of the people, the Protestant townsmen and yeoman farmers, who strive to defend their rights and privileges through Parliament. Through the ensuing struggle between Crown and Parliament the country experiences an absolute monarch, a civil war, and a dictator backed by an army—a political diversity equal to that suffered by the more unfortunate of European states some three hundred years later. The influence of the Bible, schools, and Puritanism changes the adventurous Elizabethan spirit to a more sober and responsible one. After the execution of Raleigh, Englishmen abandon piratical enterprise for peaceful penetration and colonization. Virginia is colonized and grows into a prosperous tobacco planting community, and a group of Puritans sail to America to form a new England where they can lead their conception of an ideally religious life free from persecution.

INIGO JONES • CLASSIC

The " Sovereign of the Seas," built for the Navy in 1637. Charles realizes the importance of sea power, and by means of " ship money " builds up a navy independent of the ships manned by the merchant sailors, thus separating the two marines.

Inigo Jones: the first important English architect. From now on architecture is in the hands of the individual, whose personal capabilities and tendencies are exhibited in the buildings he has designed. This individual, the architect, has a large influence on the shape and the materials of the building, and the methods of construction adopted. On his skill in planning, his sense of form, and power of selecting and using building materials, the greatness of the architecture depends.

The production of food is increased by the enclosure of common land, the draining of fens and marshes, and the improvements in design of the plough and the windmill.

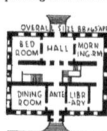

The Classic influence and altered social conditions change the house plan. The living-room, dining-room, and library have become important rooms; and the hall has shrunk to a small compartment used for the reception of guests.

Roof Types

A section through a Classic cornice, showing how the mouldings are geometrically set out. The depth of each individual moulding is to a fixed proportion, based on the diameter of the column (page 6).

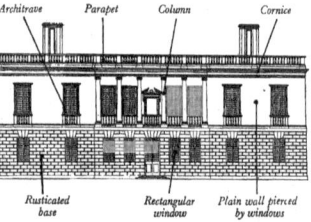

A drawing of the Queen's House at Greenwich, which explains some of the chief features of Classic architecture. The building is in itself a complete essay in design. Its elements are symmetrically disposed about an imaginary centre line. The walls have a base of thick jointed stonework which emphasizes that they carry the weight of the floors and roof. The windows are smaller in area than the wall. The building is finished at the top with a cornice, the projecting mouldings of which form a strong horizontal line.

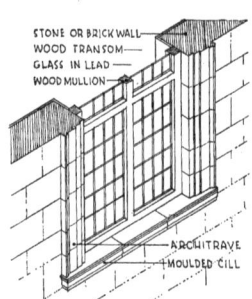

The wall and window. The wall of Classic architecture carries the weight and is unbuttressed. This limits the size of the window, which becomes a hole pierced through the wall. The window opening is usually surrounded by a Classic moulding, called an architrave, and the window itself is of wood with one mullion and a transome placed about two-thirds of the way up the height. The opening portion is an iron casement glazed with leaded lights (glass in small squares with lead canes).

CLASSIC

Classic architecture is chiefly concerned with form. The designer works to certain formal canons of art, the essentials of which are order and proportion (page 6). A Classic building is the product of one mind, the design is complete in itself, no part may be added and no part may be taken away without spoiling the proportions and, therefore, the building as a Classic work of art. Whereas the Gothic building arose from the exploitation of the peculiarities of the materials, the Classic building is erected to a preconceived design, in which the construction and materials are secondary.

BUILDING ACTIVITY. The building of large mansions by the aristocracy continues. The Crown has ambitious building programmes, but Parliament's control of the purse strings prevents their realization. Of the huge palace of Whitehall, all that is built is the Banqueting Hall. • **ARCHITECTURAL CHARACTER**: *Classic.* Inigo Jones and his followers design in the manner of the Italian architect Palladio, and because of this their work is often called " Palladian." Full use is made of the Classic elements, the plinth or base, column, crowning cornice, and rectangular windows and doors surrounded by architraves, 26. The verticality of the Elizabethan gable is replaced by the straight wall crowned by the strong horizontal line of the cornice. Roofs are hipped, 27, and are sometimes hidden by parapets, and the large built-up window is abandoned for small rectangular ones set in a large wall space. Jones's love for Palladio's work results in the use of plaster, marble, and paint for interiors rather than the traditional material, oak. He uses white plaster panelling with applied gilded ornament and introduces painted ceilings. His pupil, Webb, uses wood panelling left in its natural state, but the panels themselves are much larger than have hitherto been used, and he introduces a dado, 28, and page 26. • **BUILDINGS TO SEE.** By Jones: St. Paul's, Covent Garden; Wilton House, Salisbury. John Webb, his pupil: Thorpe Hall, Peterborough, 27, 28.

27. *Thorpe Hall, near Peterborough.* 1656. *Architect: Webb.*

26. *Queen's House, Greenwich.* 1635. *Architect: Inigo Jones.*

Inigo Jones introduces the Italian Classic manner of building in all its academic formality, 26, and architectural design returns to the static wall pierced by windows. The irregular sky-line of the Elizabethan gable is replaced by the strong horizontality of the projecting cornice, 26, and windows have shrunk to comparatively small rectangles surrounded by architraves, 27.

28. *Thorpe Hall, near Peterborough.* 1656.

12TH TO 18TH CENTURIES   THE COTTAGE

Until the Industrial Revolution, England is an agricultural country mainly populated by rural workers. When the serfs of Norman England had won their independence they became the yeoman farmers. These men form the backbone of the community until they are deprived of their share of the common land and their small holdings by the big landowners. The yeoman may be defined as "he who cultivates the ground and is independent." Not all yeomen are freeholders, however, and many supplement their earnings by working part time for the gentry. Nevertheless, no one can deprive them of their lands and, therefore, their livings, which are secure, unlike those of the industrial workers. The yeomen are kept busy from morning to night cultivating their strips of the common ground or tending their cattle on the heath. The food they produce is primarily for their own consumption; the surplus is sold to buy the things they cannot make. Their existence, centred round the village, is essentially local. Travel is arduous and their actual experience of the world is confined to the radius of a few miles. Most of them are uneducated, and their amusements are provided by the traditional feasts, fairs, and village games. The intensity of their religious belief can be judged by the countless parish churches in the country (page 16). This simplicity of life, together with its independence, produces a hardy stock with an intense love of the soil, a love of freedom, and a suspicion of any innovation. Through the comparative isolation of the villages there grows up in each a body of craftsmen who earn their living by supplying the needs of the yeomen. Although the blacksmith, carpenter, and other village craftsmen have the simplest of tools and know only laborious hand methods, they build up a tradition of craftsmanship without equal.

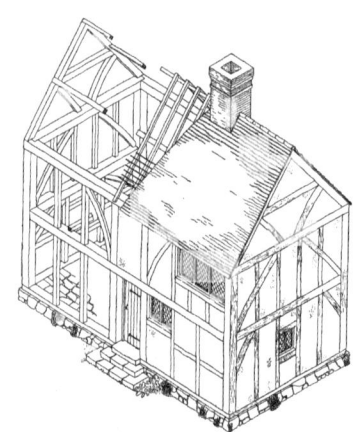

The cottage and farm is built by local craftsmen out of material found at hand. The geology of the district determines the materials used, making a close affinity between the cottage and the countryside surrounding it. The simplest possible constructional system for these materials is used, as there is no machinery, building being "by hand and hammer" to rule of thumb methods. The builders have no theories on architectural design, but just solve the problem of providing shelter for man, beast, and stores in the most direct manner. The diagram above shows a timber-framed cottage. The weight of the roof and first floor is carried by a framework of wood; the space between the members being filled in by lath and plaster or brickwork. The rectangles formed by the members of the frame are cross-braced to form triangles, making the structure absolutely rigid.

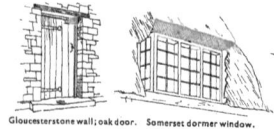      

Gloucesterstone wall; oak door.   Somerset dormer window.   Suffolk oak ceiling.   Iron casement   Iron hinge.   Heating.   Lighting.   Sanitation.

ARCHITECTURAL CHARACTER: The chief characteristics of the cottage are informality and use of local materials. The cottages are, for the most part, exceptionally small buildings, sometimes of one, but usually two storeys in height. On the ground floor is a living-room, entered directly from the outside, and wash and store houses, with bedrooms on the first floor. For the sake of economy the rooms are low; those on the first floor are partially in the roof space. The low building that results, together with the use of local materials, make the buildings appear to be part of, and to grow out of, the landscape. Constructionally they can be roughly divided into those in which the weight of the roof and first floor is carried on a solid wall, 29, and those in which it is carried by a timber frame. The weight-carrying type are mainly of stone, and the framed type of oak with the space between the members filled in with wattle and clay, brick, or lath and plaster. Roofs are of steep pitch so that the water runs quickly off them, and are covered with slate, tile, stone, or thatch. Windows are small, as glass is expensive, and they often project into the roof (dormers). They are placed in any suitable position. The first floor is of boards on wood joists, and the ground floor of clay, stone, or brick. Equipment is of the simplest kind, the fire being replenished from the nearby wood, and the water drawn from a well or spring. Barns have oak roof trusses with walls of wood boards, brick, or stone, and roofs of tile, slate, or thatch. Their long and broad roofs often come down to the ground and give an impression of great breadth and repose. ● BUILDINGS TO SEE. In each county will be found cottages exhibiting local characteristics.

29. Cottage at Cherhill, Wiltshire.

17TH CENTURY • 1660-1700   WREN • CLASSIC

1660 Charles II. -65 to 66 Plague and Fire. -79 Habeas Corpus. -85 James II. -88 William and Mary. -94 Formation of Bank of England. ● The repressive and rigid moral code of the Puritans is lifted by the restoration of Charles II, and the people once more enjoy themselves as they wish. Although in the reaction against Puritanism religious meetings are forbidden, the cult has a deep and sobering influence on the national character. With the decline of the power of the Crown comes the rise of the City merchants. No longer governed by the restrictive regulations of the medieval corporate state, or at the mercy of an absolute monarch, they are free to develop trade with every nation. They begin to build up the foreign trade that is to mean so much to the prosperity of the next century. The population of the country has now grown to over five millions, and there is an advancement of general well-being; particularly in London. In the country the poor communications and the scarcity of books retard the development of the squire and parson in politics, art, and learning. At the close of the century the conflict between King and Parliament is finally settled when the throne is accepted by the Protestant William of Orange on terms laid down by Parliament. Henceforth, no king attempts to govern in defiance of Parliament. The Dutch king seeks English support for his struggle against the Catholic Louis XIV. At the close of the century national administration is improved by an Act which requires Parliament to be summoned every three years, and the formation of the Bank of England.

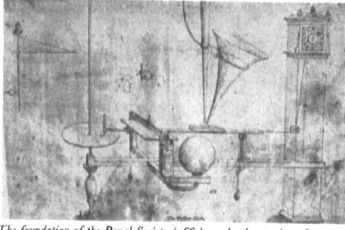

Sir Christopher Wren is an astronomer and mathematician of repute before his appointment by Charles as Assistant Surveyor - General in 1662. Evidence of his scientific mind can be seen in most of his work. His structural ingenuity in the use of the dome, the basic geometric forms of his steeples and his masterly use of building material, all reveal an intellectual approach to architectural design. But science alone does not provide fine architecture, and Wren's greatness rests in his ability to combine a purely intellectual approach to architectural problems with an intuitive sense of form. In other words, not only does he work out the most effective method of construction and select the right materials for the job, but he chooses and uses them in such a way that the form of the building, the colour and texture of its materials co-operate to make a perfectly balanced and æsthetically satisfying whole.

The foundation of the Royal Society (1663) marks the opening of a great age of scientific discovery. Wren, as a doctor of medicine and professor of astronomy, is a foundation member. His model of a weather clock, above, and the construction of the dome of St. Paul's Cathedral, below, are typical of his inventive genius and love of scientific experiment.

Communications. The maintenance of the roads is now left to the parishes. This consequent neglect makes communication difficult and prevents manufacturers from being any distance from the sea. Six horses are necessary to pull family coaches or wagons through the mud; but the first stage coaches are run on those few roads with reasonable surfaces.

Panelling: two or three planks of wood are now joined together to form wide panels; these are held in the frame by Classic mouldings.

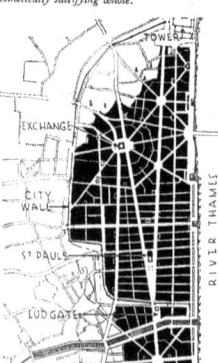

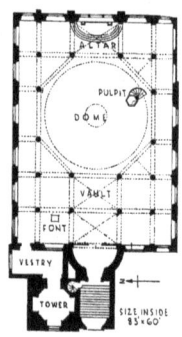

Wren is compelled to build his churches on small sites, often of awkward shapes. The plan, right, of St. Stephen's, Walbrook, is a typical example of his planning ingenuity. As Protestantism has made the reading and interpretation of the Bible of more importance than ritual, his churches are of simple geometric shapes where everyone can see the preacher. Left, Wren's sketch plan for the City in the Classic manner, with wide straight street dividing the area into rectangles bisected by radials. Important positions are reserved for public buildings which are seen down enormous vistas. The autocratic powers that make such a plan possible do not exist and the city is rebuilt on the lines of the mediæval one. But improvements are made in planning and construction; the new city being expressive of its business and residential functions.

BUILDING ACTIVITY. The destruction of London by the Fire gives Wren the opportunity to erect St. Paul's Cathedral and fifty-three City churches. The patronage of the Crown enables him to extend Hampton Court Palace and build the Orangery at Kensington. As a result of naval development he designs Greenwich Hospital, a home for old seamen. Wren is also responsible for domestic and new university buildings. ● ARCHITECTURAL CHARACTER: *Classic.* The period is so dominated by the work of Wren that it is named after him; furthermore, this title serves to differentiate the English character of the building from the Italian manner of Jones and his followers. Wren's masterly use of English materials, such as Portland stone, red brick, tiles, slates, lead, wrought iron, and wood gives the Classic style a national character, 32. His constructive and inventive genius, particularly in the case of domes and steeples, 30, 31, has a profound and lasting impression on design. In his larger and more important buildings he makes full use of Classic features, such as domes and columns for architectural emphasis; cornices for the junction of walls and roofs; and architraves around door and window. He uses both round and square-headed openings for windows and doors, and adopts the new sash window (page 28) for his domestic buildings. Craftsmen now execute details in correct, but highly decorative designs; typical of such are the wood carvings of Gibbons and the wrought iron of Tijou at St. Paul's and the City churches. Walls are lined on the inside with oak panelling or plaster, and ceilings by heavily moulded and decorated plaster. ● BUILDINGS TO SEE. By Wren: The City churches; St. Paul's Cathedral; Pembroke Chapel and Trinity Library, Cambridge; Sheldonian Theatre and Queen's Library, Oxford; Greenwich and Chelsea Hospitals.

31. Model of Wren's favourite design for St. Paul's Cathedral.

30. St. Bride's, Fleet Street. 1680. Architect: Wren.

Wren takes the traditional English building materials such as slate, warm red bricks, Portland stone, wood, and iron and, designing in the Classic manner, creates a purely national type of Classic architecture, 32. Evidence of his intellectual and scientific rather than academic approach to design can be seen in the basic geometric forms of his work, 30, 31.

32. Morden College, Blackheath. 1695. Architect: Wren.

18TH CENTURY • 1700-60

1702-Anne -07 Union with Scotland. -13 Treaty of Utrecht. -14 George I. -20 South Sea Bubble. -27 George II. -45 Jacobite Rebellion. -56 to -63 Seven Years' War. -57 Plassey. -59 Quebec.
● England is now run by the land-owning gentry. The House of Lords contains the peers and bishops, and the Commons the squires, who, by the system of election—free seats, bribery, and local influence —are automatically returned. This system, although not democratic, works very well, as England is primarily an agricultural country. The country gentry being in close contact with the people share their problems and represent their interests. The two-party system flourishes, the Puritans or Dissenters now being called the Whigs and the Cavaliers or Jacobites the Tories. The Hanoverian, George I., cannot speak English or understand our customs, and so the power of

EARLY GEORGIAN • CLASSIC

the monarchy declines. The pacific administration of Walpole, the first Prime Minister, and the failure of the Jacobite rebellion strengthens the country's faith in the Government and encourages the City trader and speculator. Interdependent with the trade expansion is the remarkable growth of the Empire. France is England's commercial and naval rival, and there is a continual struggle between the two countries in their colonial expansion. By the end of the Seven Years' War England has acquired most of the trading posts and colonies established by Europeans in America, Asia, and Africa. There are notable improvements in agriculture. Turnips are introduced as food for cattle, thus keeping them alive in winter. Townsend introduces the four-course system of rotation and Bakewell the selective breeding of cattle, whilst Tull invents a mechanical seed-sowing drill.

The field, instead of being left fallow for one year in three, is used to produce turnips. Cattle when turned into it not only manure the soil and give more meat and milk, but are kept alive during winter. Thus, fresh meat instead of salted can be had all the year round. The agricultural prosperity leads to the building of new farms, cottages and barns.

Glasgow in 1753. Agricultural developments and trading restrictions between England and Scotland are removed by the Union, and the Clyde becomes a centre for trade with America.

Warm drinks—tea, chocolate, coffee—are now a fashionable substitute for beer. Coffee houses become the meeting place of politicians, wits and intellectuals. They become more and more exclusive until they develop into clubs and business exchanges, such as White's Club and Lloyd's.

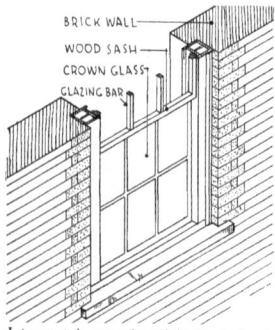

Improvements in construction and the almost universal use of brick allow the wall to be thinner. Bricks of darker colour are used to emphasize the window opening instead of the more elaborate architrave and cornice. Sash windows are in general use. Improvements in glass-making allow larger and better quality sheets to be produced. The lead cane, no longer necessary, is abandoned. The sash (sliding portion) consists of a wood frame and glazing bars dividing the window into rectangles to take the glass.

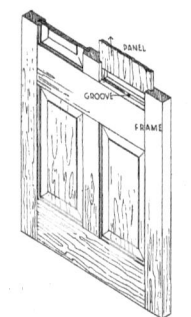

The seventeenth- and eighteenth-century panelled door; designed to correct the tendency of large pieces of wood to shrink and swell. The thin panels contract or expand in grooves in the frame. The panels are emphasized by moulding the frame; thus, the decoration arises from the structural system. The panelling of the walls of rooms is to exactly the same system.

The passion of the aristocracy for Classic architecture is seen in the many grandiose mansions built for their distinction. The favourite type of plan is a large centre block, approached by steps and monumental portico, with symmetrical low wings on either side, giving the centre great scale. As can be seen, above, from the arrangement of the Kitchen and Dining-room at Holkham Hall, Norfolk, by Kent, comfort and convenience are sacrificed for architectural effect.

BUILDING ACTIVITY. Domestic, collegiate, and ecclesiastical buildings are all erected. The aristocracy vie with each other in building magnificent country mansions. Trade expansion and the increasing responsibility of Government departments lead to the erection of Town Halls, Corn Exchanges, and Customs Houses.
● ARCHITECTURAL CHARACTER: *Classic*. The proportions and elements of Classic architecture are now applied to buildings of all sizes and types, 33, 34, 36. The larger buildings reflect the personalities of the architects who designed them, but all of them show the influence of either Jones or Wren. Thus, William Kent designs in the severe Palladian manner of Jones. Vanbrugh favours the monumental and florid type of Italian Renaissance architecture, 36. Gibbs' City churches are often mistaken for Wren's but his

Radcliffe Camera at Oxford is an ingenious and personal design. In the mansions of the aristocracy classical correctness and monumental architecture are considered more important than comfort and convenience. But common sense prevails in the smaller houses, the designs consisting of simple rectangular shapes with plain brick walls, sash windows, and elegant entrance doors, 34 and page 32. Although details are inclined to be heavy and bold in design they are simpler than those of the Wren period. ● BUILDINGS TO SEE. Castle Howard, Yorkshire, by Vanbrugh; Holkham Hall, Norfolk, and Horse Guards, Whitehall, by Kent; St. George's, Bloomsbury, by Hawksmoor; St. George's, Hanover Square, by Jones; St. Martin-in-the-Fields and Radcliffe Camera, by Gibbs.

33. St. Philip's, Birmingham. 1711–19.
Architect: T. Archer.

35. Parlour at 99, Great Russell Street, London. Early 18th century.

The Anglicized Classic manner of building evolved by Wren has now developed into the Georgian style. Although different buildings exhibit the personalities of their designers, the style is a consistent manner of building applied to all the requirements of the time, 33, 34, 37, 41, just as Gothic had been in medieval times. The aristocracy favour the more academically correct Italian Classic and sacrifice comfort and homeliness for architectural effect. 36.

34. House in Queen Anne's Gate, London. 1705.

36. Blenheim Palace, Oxfordshire. 1705. Architect: Vanbrugh.

18TH CENTURY • 1760-1800

1760 George III. –64 Hargreave's spinning jenny. –65 Stamp Act. –76 American Independence. –84 Mail coaches. –89 French Revolution. –93 Napoleonic Wars. –95 Cape of Good Hope captured.
● In America the original Puritan colonists have been followed by Quakers and Catholics until there are thirteen states, with a white population of nearly two millions. England considers that America should help to pay for the Seven Years' War, and her imposition of taxation leads to revolution and the foundation of the United States of America. The horrors of the French Revolution retard political progress in this country and bring about an exaggerated respect for everything that is old-established. Almost unnoticed a revolution of even greater consequence has started in England. This, the Industrial Revolution, is destined to change England from an

LATE GEORGIAN • CLASSIC

agricultural to an industrial country. It commences with a few seemingly unimportant inventions: mechanical methods of spinning and weaving cloth begin to replace hand production; a new puddling process is invented, by which iron can be smelted by coal instead of wood; and in steam a new source of power is discovered. Industry moves from the forests of the South to the new coalfields of the North and begins a rapid expansion. The application of the agricultural innovations of the beginning of the century increases the production of corn and cattle for consumption by the now rapidly growing population. The new farming methods can only be applied on a comparatively large scale and, in consequence, landowners buy out small holders, who then drift into the towns for employment.

James Watt improves the steam engine, and industry begins to adopt this new form of power.

The Promenade in St. James's Park in 1790.

A colonial empire demands a strong navy to protect its shores and trade routes. An efficient English fleet and the skill of commanders such as Nelson prevent England from becoming part of the Napoleonic Empire.

A ceiling designed by the Adam brothers. A typical example of Adam decoration; delicate shallow mouldings, fan-shaped ribs and flat plaques, all executed in hard plaster.

The country gentry, enriched through land enclosure and new farming methods, improve their estates by laying them out with clumps of trees, hedgerows and even artificial lakes. Thus, eighteenth-century man at not God, as was later suggested, creates what is termed " the typical English countryside." The drawing above is part of a design for a 60-acre park by an amateur landscape gardener. The formal symmetrical arrangement of the beginning of the century has been abandoned for a naturalistic but, nevertheless, carefully studied design.

With the adoption of coal for heating instead of logs of wood the fireplace becomes smaller. The fuel is contained within a basket grate, and this, together with the general improvement in design, allows less heat to go up the chimney and less smoke to enter the room. The surround of the above fireplace consists of Ionic columns surmounted by an architrave, frieze, and cornice.

BUILDING ACTIVITY. There is a continuation of the same building types of the beginning of the century, but fewer churches and large mansions are erected. As a result of British supremacy at sea, great ranges of sail lofts and warehouses are built in harbours such as Poole, Boston, and Portsmouth. A new architectural type is evolved in the exclusive London club buildings demanded by fashionable society. ● ARCHITECTURAL CHARACTER: *Classic*. Simplified Georgian Classic is now used for all buildings, excepting those few where civic dignity demands a more monumental type. The style becomes continuously more refined and simple with the increasing skill of the designer and craftsmen. The panels of doors and wood wall coverings become larger and the mouldings more refined. The boxes of sash windows are concealed in the brick walls and their glazing bars become slighter. Heavy cornices are replaced by bands of stone or slight projections. Wrought-iron railings, lamp standards, and staircase balustrades are exceptionally delicate. Of the work of the architects that of Robert and James Adam makes the greatest impression on the trend of design; particularly in interior decoration. Their work is conspicuous for its elegance and lightness, 40. They abandon the more rigid and rectangular Classic forms for curves and ellipses; their favourite features being flat elliptical or curved arches, circular and oval ends to rooms; semicircular niches and elliptical or circular plaques as wall decoration. The Adam Brothers evolved a new type of decoration based on ancient Etruscan, which they used in interior decoration as a relief for broad plain plaster surfaces. The chief characteristics are low relief painted panels, thin cobweb-like lines of decoration, and flat fan-shaped ribs, all executed in hard plaster. ● BUILDINGS TO SEE. Prior Park, Bath, by John Wood; and Somerset House, London, by Sir William Chambers, are both in the more academic and classically correct manner. Bedford Square by Thomas Leverton. The work of the Adam Brothers may be seen at Kenwood, Highgate; Lansdowne House, Berkeley Square; Stowe, Bucks; and Adam Street, Adelphi, London.

37. *Shop Front, the Haymarket, London. Late 18th Century.*

39. *The Crescent, Bath.* 1767. *Architect: Wood, the Younger.*

40. *Lansdowne House, London.* 1765. *Architects: Adam Brothers.*

38. *The Georgian development of Bath.*

The most obvious characteristics of the Georgian style are plain red brick walls and windows with painted wood glazing bars, 37, 41, 42. The Adam brothers introduce a refined type of Classic ornament which is typical of the social elegance of the time, 40. But in utilitarian structures all ornament is suppressed, the design relying for its effect on the choice of materials and Classic proportions. Georgian culture and civic pride is responsible for the development of towns in an ordered and planned manner, 38. Houses are grouped together in the form of terraces, and are arranged round open spaces planted with grass and trees.

41. *Warehouse at Portsmouth Dockyard.* 1771.

18TH CENTURY

In spite of the agricultural and industrial revolutions the eighteenth century is one of calm individualism. The bitter political and religious strife of the last century dies under an obviously stable constitutional monarchy and a tolerant Church of England. The country is run by a land-owning aristocracy, and until towards the end of the century, the mass of the people are engaged in agriculture under the direction and care of the local gentry and parson. The wise political administration of Walpole and Pitt, colonial and commercial expansion, and agricultural improvements, advance the general standard of living. Amongst the privileged class there is a craze for the culture and learning of Classic antiquity. Translations of the great Greek and Roman authors are read as avidly as the newspapers, and every gentleman of quality makes it his business to be thoroughly conversant with the principles of Classic architecture (pages 6 and 22). Many books are published on architecture, giving

THE GEORGIAN HOUSE • CLASSIC

details of the Orders (page 6) and designs for such features as windows, doorways, and fire-places; and many architects and their patrons visit Italy and study the ancient and Renaissance buildings at first hand. Manners and dress are conspicuous for their fastidious elegance. The professional classes and the clergy take their cue from the aristocracy, upon whom they are dependent. The craftsman is brought up in a sound tradition, in which Classic forms have been adapted and nationalised for contemporary articles. His work is unhurried and free from advertising campaigns and price-cutting. His customer knows what he wants and appreciates it when he gets it. The result of all this is that in Georgian England no ugly article is produced. Whether it is a town hall or a tea-pot the same care is taken in the design and execution, and the same cultural background is evident in both articles.

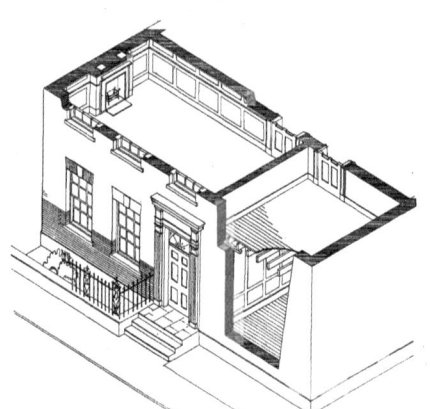

The keen civic sense of landlord and architect is responsible for the development of towns in an ordered and properly planned manner. The town house is thought of as a unit in the general design of the street, and not as a monument to the virtuosity of the builder or the pocket of the owner. The design is by an architect who recognises only one manner of building, the Classic; his patron is fully acquainted with the principles of this architecture, and the builder, should he be required to design, has at his disposal the "pattern books" in which are set out designs for doors, fire-places, and the other elements. The diagram above shows the construction of a Georgian house. Brick walls of standard thicknesses carry the weight of the floors and roof, and distribute it along a continuous foundation. Wood floor joists span from wall to wall, the structural qualities of this material limiting the size of the rooms and necessitating thick weight-carrying walls inside the building. Windows are also limited in size, as there must always be a mass of material in the walls to support the floors.

   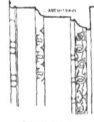  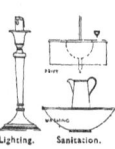

Door and case. Sash window and panelling. Wrought iron. Staircase. Ornament. Heating. Lighting. Sanitation.

ARCHITECTURAL CHARACTER: *Classic*, but so nationalised that it is called the Georgian style. Simple plans, evolved through the use of weight-carrying brick walls, timber floors and roofs, in Classic proportions, to suit the needs of the "gentleman of quality." Elevations consist of plain brick walls with stone or brick "dressings" pierced with sash windows. They rely entirely for their effect on the proportion of the solids and voids and their relation to each other. Architectural features are confined to the entrance door and elegant wrought-iron work. Windows are of the sash variety with wood glazing bars. In the early houses the area of the wall exceeds that of the window, but as building technique improves the windows become as wide as is structurally possible with a weight-carrying wall. Doors are panelled, and, here again, as craftsmanship improves the frames get smaller and the panels larger. Throughout the century the roof gets flatter; steeply pitched tiled roofs with dormer windows and heavy cornices give way to low-pitched roofs hidden behind tall parapets. Internally the rooms are panelled in wood or plaster. Classic mouldings and decorative features are used for the details; and there is a continuous striving for simplicity and refinement. ● BUILDINGS TO SEE. Georgian houses in almost every town in the country, and, in particular, London Squares such as Hanover, Cavendish and Berkeley. These should all be seen as soon as possible, as most of them are being torn down or mutilated.

42. Opposite page: Barnfield Crescent, Exeter. 1798

19TH CENTURY • 1800-1837 REGENCY • CLASSIC

1801 Land Enclosure Act. -05 Trafalgar. -11 Prince Regent. -15 Waterloo. -20 George IV. -30 William IV. -32 Reform Bill. -34 Poor Law Act. -35 Municipal Corporations Act. ● The Industrial Revolution is now well on its way. The new mining and manufacturing towns in the North are growing ever larger, and the population has risen to twelve millions. Agriculture no longer produces enough food for the country, which, through the economic blockade during the Napoleonic Wars, is faced with starvation. A General Land Enclosure Act is passed to counteract this, and thousands of acres of common land and small holdings are attached to the big farms for the large-scale production of wheat. Agricultural workers thus deprived of their means of existence drift into the towns for employment in the factories, and those who manage to keep their land, unable to compete with the new farming methods, are driven to poverty. The countryside is changing in appearance from the traditional open common and waste lands into well-cultivated fields and pastures divided up by hedges and fences. The miserable condition to which the agricultural worker has been driven is matched by that of the worker in the mines and factories. In addition the workers are badly hit by taxes on every-day goods, in particular, that on imported corn. The right of a few privileged landowners to conduct the affairs of the country is questioned by the new urban population and by social reformers. The voice of political reform is raised, and the aristocracy finds itself fighting with its back to the wall to preserve its ancient privileges and rights. At length, after a fierce struggle, the Reform Bill is passed giving votes to the small property owners, thus making Parliament more truly representative. The new Parliament sets to work and passes a series of Acts, which improve working conditions in the factories, give assistance to the poor, and reform government in the towns.

Carlton House Terrace in the early nineteenth century.

Horse buses are first seen in London. Telford and Macadam are improving roads, and a new form of communication, the canal, carries coal and heavy goods for the new industries.

John Nash (1752-1835), *the outstanding architect of the Regency period. He excels rather as a man of affairs, a contriver, than as a man of great intellect. He has the driving force to realize his ambitious projects, and to this end he finances and launches building schemes, entertains lavishly, and eventually becomes architect to the Prince Regent. Nash concerns himself with broad architectural effects rather than with the perfection of detail. He designs, not only in terms of whole groups of buildings, but in that of avenues, colonnades, roads, paths, trees, and grass as well ; in fact he is a Town Planner.*

Plan of a detached house of 1830, such as that shown in 44, on the facing page. A compact orderly arrangement with well-proportioned rooms and a minimum of wasted space.

The discoveries of archaeologists in Greece bring to light the Classic architecture of that country, and Greek decorative features, such as the anthemion or honeysuckle ornament, above, become fashionable.

THE PATENT KITCHENER.

New types of iron ranges with ovens, hot-plate, and sometimes a water heater, are put in the houses springing up in the suburbs. They and the coal fires in the living-rooms are to be largely responsible for the smoke and soot of the big nineteenth-century cities. Above : an example made in 1829.

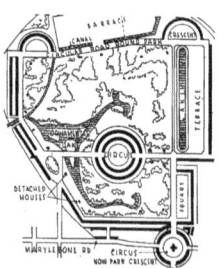

Nash's plan for Regent's Park is a scheme for turning the existing fields and scattered farms on the North side of the town into a residential zone for the aristocracy. The Park is surrounded by a drive and imposing blocks of terrace houses. It is laid out in the romantic manner with trees and lakes, amongst which are disposed forty or fifty detached houses. At the main approach from Portland Place is a circus, and in the centre another circus with houses looking outwards into the Park.

BUILDING ACTIVITY. George IV, aided by Nash, amuses himself by building a succession of homes. Terraces of houses are erected in towns like Leamington and Brighton, due to the now fashionable sea bathing and taking of spa waters. In the industrial North, speculators discover a lucrative business in building potential slums for workers. ● ARCHITECTURAL CHARACTER: *Classic.* The unrest and conflicting social forces at work deflect architecture into different channels. The aristocracy is still powerful enough to direct taste, and Georgian architecture reaches its final expression in the Regency style. But the new industries in the North and the new inventions are beginning to produce an altogether different form of building. The Prince Regent, as self-styled " First Gentleman of Europe," is the cultured representative of the period, which is therefore named after him. The most obvious characteristic of Regency architecture is painted stucco, that is, the hard plaster with which the whole of the exteriors of the buildings are finished. Although the usual Classic features are still in use, 43, the buildings have a simpler appearance than those of the last century, due to the plain painted surfaces and the use of refined Greek ornament. Flat segmental bay windows become popular, and glazed casement doors are used as well as the sash; in small houses windows are set straight into plain walls with no surface decoration such as architraves, 44. The use of slate allows a still lower roof pitch, and in some of Nash's work it becomes quite flat. The eaves to the small houses are boldly projecting to form a strong contrast to the plain walls. Balconies, a new feature of domestic design, are supported on brackets of slender columns of iron or stone. The Georgian tradition of design is abandoned for houses built for the industrial workers in the North. As profit is the only incentive, they are little more than long rows of brick cells, 45. No conveniences are provided, and there is a minimum of light and air. ● BUILDINGS TO SEE. The terraces in the proximity of Regent's Park, by Nash. Houses and terraces in Brixton, Cheltenham, Bath, Leamington, Brighton, Weymouth, Ramsgate, and Dover.

Georgian architecture reaches its final expression in the Regency period. An exceptional purity of design is attained by the use of flat painted stucco walls, sash windows with thin wood members, broadly projecting eaves, and elegant balconies, 44. Nash plans a magnificent residential district for the aristocracy in London, stretching from Regent's Park in the north to Carlton House Terrace in the south, 43. But in the North of England Georgian culture is dead and the houses erected for the industrial workers have no hygienic, let alone architectural, qualities, 45.

43. *Carlton House Terrace.* 1827. Architect: Nash.

44. *A House at Brixton. Early 19th Century.*

45. *Houses in the Industrial North.*

19TH CENTURY • 1837-1900

1837 Victoria. –46 Repeal of Corn Laws. –57 Indian Mutiny. –67 Second Reform Bill. –70 Education Act. –84 Third Reform Bill. –85 Khartoum. –89 County Councils Act. –94 Parish Councils Act. • Through parliamentary reform, the industrial middle classes —the wealthy ironmaster, millowner, shopkeeper—obtain control of the country from the land-owning aristocracy. Having the interests of the town dweller or industrialist at heart rather than the farmer, they repeal the Corn Laws and similar taxes on imported foodstuffs. In consequence, industry advances rapidly at the expense of agriculture. Under the doctrine of "laissez-faire," or each man for himself and the devil take the hindermost, there is unlimited scope for private enterprise in commerce. In the ever-expanding colonial and foreign markets and the increasing population at home, there is a consumer who can absorb all that the new industrial machine can produce. Steam and iron make possible the railway

VICTORIAN • REVIVALS

era and a mercantile marine that becomes the carrier for the world. Improvements in mining and weaving expand the coal and clothing industries to an undreamt-of size. The practical application of a host of inventions creates new industries and adds to the material advantages at the disposal of the community. Abroad, the Government takes over control of India and the Suez Canal. British influence is extended in Egypt, and in the scramble in the Far East and Africa large territories are added to the British Empire. The lesson of the American colonies has been learnt and self-government is given to Canada and the Australian Commonwealth. This is a period of extraordinary prosperity for the upper and middle classes; but not for the lower. The squalor, filth and ignorance in which the teeming masses live and work excite the compassion of social reformers, and the conscience of the public is pricked sufficiently to bring about a series of factory, education, and health Acts.

Ornament has been in the past a means of emphasizing the shapes and the structural qualities of objects. Now it is an end in itself, and confuses rather than defines the shape. The object of the designs is to make a show; meaningless decoration is preferred to beauty of form. The clock above and the house below on the right are typical examples of what is termed "applied" decoration—decoration on an object rather than of it.

A scene in the Great Exhibition, London, 1851.

A bath heated by gas. Sanitation is improved by the introduction in the home of such equipment as the bath, lavatory basin and w.c., and by the installation of communal drainage and water systems.

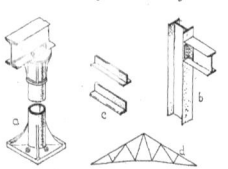

Some new building units : a, cast-iron column, superseded by the rolled steel joist used as a column, b, and to which further joists are riveted to form a rigid framework ; c, steel angles and tees used to build light big span roof trusses, d.

House Plan, 1870. The middle class ape their superiors ; they must have a multitude of rooms to express their social standing. But as the house is on a smaller scale, and as its shape is practically determined by the elevations, these rooms are small and crowded together with numerous internal walls, making the arrangement of the house unnecessarily complex.

The Regency terrace houses deteriorate into the dull and pompous Early Victorian terraces with pretentious entrance porticos and enormous basements housing the unfortunate domestics. But with the rise of individualism and decline of the civic sense, the terrace is abandoned for the individual house. The architect of the house above described it as displaying "splendid confusion and the triumph of the picturesque."

Georgian culture loses its influence as the industrial middle classes supplant the aristocracy. With profit as the chief motive for human existence, the industrialists turn the towns of England, and therefore the material surroundings of the people, into places of squalor and dirt. Architects are repulsed by the new conditions ; and iron, steel, plate glass, and other materials that are used by industry become associated in their minds

REVIVALS

with ugliness. Encouraged by sociologists and writers, such as John Ruskin, they turn with longing to the past, when architecture and art were a part of everyday existence (page 12). Instead of taking the new materials and processes and making with them an architecture suitable for the changed conditions, they begin to revive past styles. Architecture becomes separated from engineering and degenerates into a

method of ornamentation ; the architect is only employed when civic or individual pride demands something more than a purely utilitarian structure. Architecture becomes an exclusive profession ; and its leaders favour either the revival of Gothic or Classic forms. The competition between the exponents of the two styles becomes so keen that it is called "the Battle of the Styles."

BUILDING ACTIVITY. A rapidly increased population causes the erection of houses, shops, and offices by the thousand. Social reform Acts and a religious revival stimulate the erection of Town Halls, libraries, schools, churches and chapels. • ARCHITECTURAL CHARACTER : Revivals. Owing to the separation of engineering from architecture and the failure of architects to formulate a new architecture for the new social conditions, there is no consistent architectural character other than the revival of past styles. Of these the Early English Gothic is at first the most popular, but it soon degenerates into a hybrid style which no medieval designer could have produced, 49. In competition with the Gothic revival is that of Classic forms. Here, again, the style commences with archæological accuracy—Town Halls being in the form of Greek or Roman temples, 46—but it deteriorates into a method of designing elevations totally

divorced from Classic principles. Most architects design in both styles—sometimes in the same building—and, having tired of these, begin to revive Tudor, Jacobean, and even styles from other countries. Planning, convenience, and economy are sacrificed for external effects. When the new cheap materials such as glass and iron are used they are either made to look like traditional building materials or ignored as elements in the design. Walls, windows, doors, and roofs are in every conceivable shape and size, 47, 51. Ornament, which had hitherto been solely a means of defining the form of the building, is now an end in itself, 52. Decoration runs riot, and buildings are covered both inside and out with a confusion of architectural "features" invariably borrowed from some past style, and turned out mechanically by the new industrial processes. • BUILDINGS TO SEE. Examples of the Revivals can be seen in practically every town.

46. *Birmingham Town Hall.* 1834. Architect: J. A. Hansom.

49. *The Prudential, Holborn.* 1879. Architect: A. Waterhouse.

47. *The Post Office, Leeds.* 1896. Architect: H. Tanner.

50. *An Oxford Don's House.* 1865.

51. *Liverpool Offices.* 1895. Architect: N. Shaw.

48. *Nineteenth Century Urban Development.*

52. *A Late Victorian Interior.*

Architecture is now a method of dressing up important buildings. The architect looks back and begins to revive past styles, the most popular being the Gothic, 49, and the Greek or Roman Classic, 46. The decorative features of these styles are applied, often in a distorted way, 52, to buildings constructed in a quite different manner and serving altogether different purposes, 47, 51. The rich man lives in an "architect designed" detached house, 50, and the poor man in one of a row, 48. Houses are packed round the factories and strangle communications. The citizen lives in a polluted atmosphere.

19TH CENTURY

1812 First steam boat. -13 Gas lighting. -40 Penny postage. -43 Iron steamer crosses Atlantic. -44 First telegraph. -44 to -50 Railway mania. -55 Steel girders rolled for buildings. -56 Bessemer process for producing a cheap mild steel. -65 Atlantic cable. -76 Telephones. -83 Steam tonnage equals sailing tonnage. ● As we have seen, the industrial revolution commences with the application of a few simple inventions to the problems of producing cheap manufactured goods and cheap transport. The scientist, engineer, and industrialist change the traditional domestic system of production by their use of iron for making machinery, and coal for generating steam to drive it. Work in a cottage or under a "master" in his own house is replaced by the factory system, in which a large number of people are concentrated in specialised manufacture. As one improvement after another is devised for the more efficient and economical working of the mines, factories, and railways, all kinds of subsidiary industries and trades are created, bringing more and more of the population into industrial employment. The material advantages of the industrial system are that the aggregate wealth of the nation is increased by over sevenfold between 1800 and 1900; manufactured goods are brought within the means of the majority of the community instead of a chosen few; and stable employment is provided for the bulk of the people. The speeding up of the means of communication facilitates human intercourse within the country and internationally. On the other hand, agriculture begins to deteriorate. Through free trade and improvements in shipping the country finds it cheaper to import corn than to grow it; and cattle breeding declines through the invention of the refrigerator, allowing meat to be imported. Furthermore, the agricultural community becomes backward, and a stranger to the new industrial population.

ARCHITECT ENGINEERS

The introduction of coke for smelting and the invention of puddling and rolling processes enable iron to be produced on an industrial scale. When the production of iron has got well under way Bessemer invents his famous converter, which makes possible the mass production of mild steel.

After the application of steam to sailing ships comes the change from the paddle to the screw, and wood construction to iron. From the middle of the century onwards British shipping extends until it operates all over the world. The picture above of the Clyde in 1850 makes an interesting comparison with that on page 28.

The new goods have to be moved, and as horses and carts are an expensive method of transport, a network of canals is laid down. No sooner do these take traffic from the roads than the railway becomes a practical proposition and supersedes them both.

Hungerford Bridge from an early print. Right, the Great Western Railway Crumlin Viaduct.

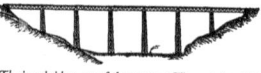

The iron bridges are of three types: The arch in which a light lattice or web of iron takes the place of the traditional massive stone arch with heavy abutments, 54; the solid girder acting as a lintel which, to save the area of metal, develops into the flat lattice (above); the suspension, in which the roadway is hung from piers by suspending chains which are anchored in the earth on either bank (left).

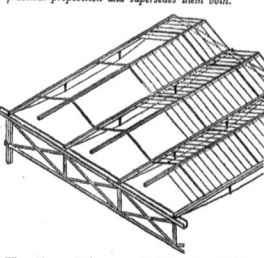

The ridge and furrow roof of the Crystal Palace. Standard beam and column sizes and a standardized glass size (49 by 10 inches) are used throughout. In place of the heavy wall of Classic architecture is thin glass to keep out the weather. The limitations are that sheet glass and iron are bad thermal insulators, making the buildings cold in winter and hot in summer.

The technical problems arising from the new industries and means of transport are solved by the engineers. With the industrialization of England the original small body that constituted the Institute of Civil Engineers grows enormously, and the engineer becomes one of the most important members of the community. As the architect became dissociated from industry (page 36), the engineers are employed to design the new building types required. Architecture and engineering are inseparable—the design of a building arises out of the structure—and the buildings must

ARCHITECT ENGINEERS

inevitably suffer when forced into two separate types, one designed by the architect and the other by the engineer. We have seen that when the architect ignored the structure, architecture degenerated; on the other hand, the engineer concerned solely with the scientific solution of the problem will produce a sound building, but not necessarily fine architecture. In all building problems the designer is given some choice of forms and materials, all of which will do the job equally well. But few engineers have the gift of choosing those shapes, textures and colours that,

combined together, will be the most beautiful; their training does not encourage it as does that of the architect. Thus, they produce fine feats of engineering, but seldom fine architecture. When the engineer is gifted with a sense of form he is an architect. During the nineteenth century a few great engineers possess this aesthetic sense, and to distinguish them from those not so gifted and from the architects who employed themselves in reviving past styles, I have called them "architect engineers."

BUILDING ACTIVITY. Improvements to communications are responsible for new architectural types in railway stations, bridges, and engine sheds. The first great exhibition hall, the Crystal Palace, is built to house the exhibition of Industrial art. ● ARCHITECTURAL CHARACTER. The most obvious characteristic is the use of iron and glass for two main building types: the big span hall, and the bridge. The railway stations and exhibition halls, under the first group, have iron arches or trusses and columns which bring the weight of the roof down to isolated points. The spaces between the iron members are filled in with sheets of glass fixed to wood or, later, metal glazing bars. Thus, both the wall and the roof become a thin skin which keeps out the weather and lets in the light. The adoption of lattice construction for trusses and arches, 53, owing to the structural rigidity of a series of members fixed in triangular shapes, makes possible the building of bridges and halls of exceptionally wide span. The new forms of construction and building types give rise to new aesthetic qualities such as the repetition of standardized units, the lace-like pattern of the criss-cross lattice construction; the enclosure of space by a transparent envelope or skin; and the sense of members in tension as against the gravitational qualities of the traditional stone pier or brick wall. ● BUILDINGS TO SEE. The station roofs of King's Cross by Cubitt, Paddington by Brunel, and St. Pancras by Barlow. The Palm House at Kew by Burton and Turner, an early iron conservatory building, of which type the Crystal Palace is a gigantic adaptation. Suspension bridges: Menai and Conway by Telford, Marlow by Clarke, and Clifton by Brunel. The first iron arched bridge at Coalbrookdale, Shropshire; Chepstow flat girder bridge by Brunel.

53. *St. Pancras Station, London.* 1868. Architect: *Barlow.*

54. *Craigellachie Bridge.* 1813. Architect: *Telford*

The architect engineers exploit the now cheap materials, iron and glass, to solve the problems arising from the Industrial Revolution, 53, 54. *They design with keenly analytical minds unencumbered by nostalgia for the past, and as many of them have an innate sense of form, they produce magnificent structures with new architectural characteristics such as the arched iron and glass roof,* 53, *the glass and iron wall,* 55, *and the sense of structural members in tension,* 54.

55. *The Crystal Palace, Sydenham.* 1854. Architect: *Paxton.*

20TH CENTURY • 1900-1909

EDWARDIAN • REVIVALS

1901 Edward VII. −02 End of Boer War. Education Act. −03 King Edward's Continental tour. Inception of Ford motor. −05 Workmen's Unemployment Bill. −09 Union of South Africa. ● The industrial machine is now accepted by all but a few of the aristocracy, and what little power remains in their hands is taken away by an Act which makes the House of Lords powerless, finally, to reject a Bill passed by the Commons. The artisan class wins still further freedom from oppression, and is becoming a vigorous and progressive section of the community. The rigorous moral code of the " middle and upper " classes is relaxing ; young people demand more freedom, and are taken out of the house by new attractions such as bicycling. Young women begin to take up other careers than that of marriage ; they go about unchaperoned, and astonish the country with the suffragette movement. The country is becoming more gay and less restrained, but there is a growing uneasiness and loss of assurance. English overseas commerce is challenged, even the colonies begin to manufacture their own goods, and countries which cannot compete with the English manufacturers erect tariff walls. In retaliation, Mr. Joseph Chamberlain preaches Tariff Reform, and Free Trade is abandoned. Education is put into the hands of the County and Borough Councils under the control of the Board of Education; and further social reforms are made through the perseverance of the new Labour members. Politically, the increasing size of the fighting forces of the now prosperous and united Germany causes uneasiness and apprehension. England, abandoning her policy of isolation, establishes friendly relationship with France. Suspicion and mistrust divide Europe into the Triple Alliance and the Triple Entente, and an arms race commences.

Cheap transport now is provided by the bicycle as well as the new electric trams, allowing the worker to live some distance from his place of work ; in consequence, the towns spread outwards in the form of large suburbs.

Piccadilly Circus in 1901. From its crude beginnings advertising is becoming the " Poor man's art gallery "; but it is also open to abuse. Elevations of buildings are let as poster hoardings, to the complete degradation of architecture. Lettering may be used in architecture, but only as an integral part of the design.

Wilbur Wright flies the first heavier-than-air machine in 1903. On the ground, machines with similar motive power are capable of travelling as fast as railway trains ; but the roads have been built for horse traffic, and to prevent the inevitable accidents a speed limit is fixed of twenty miles per hour. Above : A Farman biplane. (By courtesy of " Flight.")

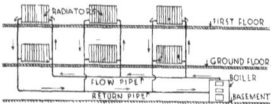

Central heating (radiators in individual rooms heated by hot water which circulates through pipes connected to a central boiler plant) provides even, constant, and clean heating, and banishes the innumerable coal fires with their individual brick flues.

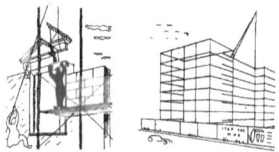

Left : traditional building by hand. Right : the new steel frame and mechanized building methods. Large buildings are now entirely supported by steel members, called rolled steel joists, riveted and bolted together to form a rigid framework. This steel frame permits lighter walls, larger windows, less weight of building material, and taller buildings with a greater capacity on a given area. The weight of the building is brought down to isolated points, giving large uninterrupted floor areas which can be divided at will by light partitions. Architects disguise the steel frame behind stone elevations which are made to look as if they carry the weight. (See facing page.)

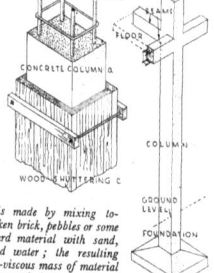

Concrete is made by mixing together broken brick, pebbles or some similar hard material with sand, cement and water ; the resulting dense semi-viscous mass of material may be poured into moulds of almost any shape and will set hard. When steel bars are embedded in the concrete it has great tensile and compressive strength, and is called Reinforced Concrete. Above on the left is a reinforced concrete column, a, with the concrete cut away to reveal the steel reinforcing rods, b. The wood shuttering, c, forms the temporary mould into which the liquid concrete is poured. The complete column with foundation and beams to carry the floors is on the right.

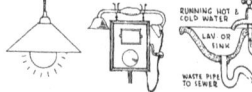

Electricity provides light without fumes or smoke which can be immediately switched on. Telephones give communication within the building or between one building and another. Plumbing services provide fresh or take away dirty water. All the above services complicate the planning and erection of the building. Although pipes and cables are draped about the building after it is erected, they are beginning to be considered as part of the design, and provision is occasionally made for properly housing them in the structure.

BUILDING ACTIVITY. Numerous banks, office buildings, theatres, hotels, churches and factories are erected. Through the high cost of land in built-up areas, large blocks of flats are built by speculators for the rich, and by voluntary housing associations for the poor. Speculative builders extend the principal cities with vast suburbs of small houses. ● ARCHITECTURAL CHARACTER : *Revivals.* The Classic Revival once again flourishes and becomes the favourite style; and office blocks and hotels vie with public buildings in their " grandeur." Characteristic of these are monumental heavily rusticated stone elevations decked out with Ionic columns, Roman armour, wreaths of flowers, and groups of statuary, 56. These features are mainly applied to the front elevations only, the backs being covered with fire stairs—now required through the increased height of buildings—and drain pipes. Correct Classic proportions are usually ignored. Through the use of the steel frame and the lift many buildings are eight storeys high, making it practically impossible to see the Classic features of the topmost storeys from the comparatively narrow streets. The Gothic Revival is still the most popular style for churches, but other styles are revived, such as the ancient Byzantine for Westminster Cathedral. A return to simplicity and honesty begins to take place in domestic architecture, the best examples being by Lethaby, Voysey, Walton, and Mackintosh. Although these architects make little use of new materials, they reject Revivalist features, and taking traditional building materials, such as brick, stone, and slate, build in the simple, straightforward traditional cottage manner, 58. Elevations have plain wall surfaces pierced with rather small windows, steep roofs, and tall chimneys. Planning is informal, but more rational than that of the Victorian house. ● BUILDINGS TO SEE. Deptford and Cardiff Town Halls ; the Central Hall, Westminster, by Lanchester and Rickards. Morning Post, Strand, by Arthur Davis. Gaiety Theatre and Piccadilly Hotel by Norman Shaw. Electric House, Moorgate, by John Belcher.

The revival of past styles continues, the most characteristic being an ornate Classic which is conspicuous for its heavy rusticated masonry. Ionic columns and groups of statuary, 56. Although the new materials and structural systems are used they are disguised by ornamental stone façades which have every appearance of carrying the weight of the building, 57. In domestic architecture there is a move towards simplification in design. Interiors become less confused, 59, and many homes are erected in the traditional cottage and farm manner of building, 58, 60.

56. *Norwich Union Insurance Society Building.* 1906. *Architects*: G. J. and F. W. Skipper.

57. *Insurance Building, Strand.* 1907. *Architect*: H. T. Hare.

59. *Brocklesby Park, Lincs.* 1901. *Architect*: Sir R. Blomfield.

58. *A House near Malvern.* 1890. *Architect*: C. F. A. Voysey.

60. "*The Orchards,*" *Godalming.* 1899. *Arch.*: Sir E. Lutyens.

20TH CENTURY • 1909-35

1910 George V. −11 National Health and Unemployment Insurance. −13 Trade Union Act. −14 to −18 Great War. −18 Women Franchise. −19 Versailles. −20 First League Assembly. −23 Economic Conference. −25 Locarno Treaty. −26 General Strike. −31 Financial Crisis. −33 Milk Marketing Scheme. ● International ambitions, suspicions and mistrust come to a head in " The War to End War " or " The War to make the World safe for Democracy." The industrial machine is dedicated to destruction, with results beyond the wildest dreams of man. The age-long desire to fly like a bird and swim like a fish is realized, and civil populations are driven underground by the aeroplane and starved by the submarine. The principles of mass production, which are to bring plenty to the world, are perfected, and shells and guns are turned out by the million. After the war the world finds itself impoverished. In many countries existing plutocratic political institutions are overthrown for social democracy, which is, in turn, replaced by dictatorial government.

GEORGE V • REVIVALS

The League of Nations is formed in order to promote international co-operation and to achieve international peace and security; but its effectiveness is reduced by the withdrawal from membership of America, and later, Germany and Japan. England is no longer the workshop of the world. European countries are too poor to import from her, America and Japan have built up enormous industrial machines and are taking English trade, and the colonies are no longer dependent on the mother country. Lack of foreign trade, machine production, and the emancipation of women swell the unemployment figures; prices rise and whole areas are stricken with depression. The standard of living of those employed is, however, steadily improving. Social services are being extended to a wider and wider sphere, mass production brings articles, hitherto considered ,luxuries, within the reach of everyone. The practical application of inventions such as the internal combustion engine, wireless, and the cinematograph, change man's habits and his material surroundings.

Mass Production. The principles of mass production bring hitherto luxury articles, such as the motor car, within the reach of a large proportion of the community.

Cheap transport changes the appearance of England. Quiet country lanes are widened, trees and hedges torn down, and petrol stations, roadhouses, and advertisement hoardings erected. The habits and manners of the people are adjusted to the new hobby of motoring. The townsman spends more time in the fresh air. The Victorian Sunday disappears, and the " middle classes " spend their week-ends in the country visiting pleasure resorts and beauty spots.

By means of the motor car the townsman discovers the countryside. But the roads have been designed for slow horse-drawn vehicles, and, in consequence, the death rate from accidents is appalling. The motorist is hampered by all kinds of restrictions, but all of no avail ; the fault is not with him. A motor car is a fast vehicle and, like the train, requires its own exclusive track.

Jazz or Modernistic. Streamlining and machine forms in transport and industry, cubist art, and the jazz mania all have a superficial effect on architecture. For example, many cinemas have enormous streamline towers or similar useless features, and are decorated inside with zig-zag and other jazz ornament. Furthermore, some architects have been attracted by the modern movement (page 46) and create over-emphasized forms in a misguided attempt to " go modern." Architecturally these manifestations are unimportant, as the form of a building should arise from its purpose and the materials in which it is constructed. 1, vertical emphasis of the form of the building; 2, horizontal emphasis obtained by alternating different coloured bands of brickwork; 3, strong contrast between horizontal and vertical; 4, Georgian type house with flat roof; 5, 6, Jazz door and decoration.

" Tooth and Gap." A residue from Victorian England, when detached houses were considered to be superior to semi-detached. Speculative builders build in the imitation Tudor cottage style, and architects in the Georgian Revival. The eighteenth-century tradition of open spaces and houses grouped together in dignified terraces is sacrificed for tiny individual dwellings with gaps between them.

Transitional. New social and building conditions create new architectural forms. These, when applied to buildings designed in the revived Wren or Georgian manner, make an architectural type which is transitional between Revivals and Modern (page 46). The twentieth-century Transitional buildings are comparable to those of the sixteenth century, when Classic forms were applied to traditional Gothic buildings. The balcony above is constructed in reinforced concrete ; the nature of this material allows it to be cantilevered straight out from the wall without vertical supports ; an entirely new structural system. The elevation from which it projects is in the Georgian Revival manner.

BUILDING ACTIVITY. Civic, commercial, and ecclesiastical buildings are erected in large numbers. New building types are evolved in the cinema and open-air swimming pools. The serious post-war housing shortage is combated by a strong housing policy, by which four million houses are erected by private enterprise or State assistance. Numerous slums are cleared and blocks of flats erected by Local Authorities. ● ARCHITECTURAL CHARACTER: *Revivals.* Economic conditions brought about by the war, and the advancement in architectural education through the establishment of schools of architecture, bring about better planning, simpler and more academically correct buildings, typical of which are revivals in the Georgian and Wren styles, 63. This simplification reaches such an extent that in many buildings all traces of Classic details have disappeared. But Classic proportions, such as the disposition of windows, are still retained, and static walls have the appearance of carrying the weight of the building—whereas, behind them is a live steel frame. The houses built with State assistance are generally simple rectangular brick boxes with pitched slate or tile roofs and small windows, the appearance being reminiscent of the English cottage, 67. Most of the houses built by private enterprise are decorated rather than designed—that is, proportion and suitability of purpose are secondary to the trimmings, such as imitation half timbering, tiles hung on bay windows, and panels of coloured cement. New features, such as cantilevered hoods and balconies, are grafted on many Revivalist buildings, making a Transitional style. The desire for streamline and jazz forms influences the design of certain buildings, particularly factories and cinemas. In such buildings the plans are the same as those decorated in the Revival manner; the introduction of the new forms being purely superficial. ● BUILDINGS TO SEE. *Georgian Revival :* banks or large houses; Rectangular *Cottage* type houses ; semi-detached speculative builders' houses; *Transitional* commercial buildings and Modernistic cinemas.

61. *Bush House, London.* 1923. Architects: *Helmle and Corbett.*

62. *Regal Theatre, Sunderland.* 1932. Architects: *Gray and Evans.*

63. *Flats, St. John's Wood.* 1937. Architects: *Wimperis, Simpson and Guthrie.*

64. *Flats at Ealing, London.* 1935. Architects: *Toms and Partners.*

65. *Liberty's, London.* 1924. Architects: *E. T. and S. Hall.*

66. *Typical speculative suburban dwellings.* 1918-38.

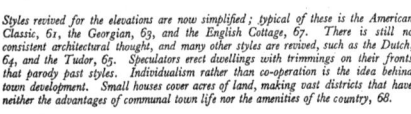

67. *Housing scheme, Welwyn, Herts.* 1937. Architect: *G. Barnsley.*

Styles revived for the elevations are now simplified; typical of these is the American Classic, 61, the Georgian, 63, and the English Cottage, 67. There is still no consistent architectural thought, and many other styles are revived, such as the Dutch, 64, and the Tudor, 65. Speculators erect dwellings with trimmings on their fronts that parody past styles. Individualism rather than co-operation is the idea behind town development. Small houses cover acres of land, making vast districts that have neither the advantages of communal town life nor the amenities of the country, 68.

68. *Housing scheme in Essex.*

20TH CENTURY
THE MODERN DWELLING

The material progress made in England during the first third of the twentieth century has exceeded all that was attained in past centuries from the Norman Conquest until the Victorian era. The inventions and discoveries that have had practical application for everyday use are innumerable. The motor-cycle, artificial silk, neon lighting, stainless metals, and fountain-pens are but a few random items in a list that is almost endless. With the material progress come great social changes, with the result that man today can live a much fuller life in an altogether wider world. These changes are having a marked influence on the design of everyday things and, in a lesser degree, on the design of dwellings. We have seen that after the Georgian tradition broke down, art became separated from industry and the machines were used for producing goods that were vulgar imitations of past styles. Although this practice still continues, an attempt is being made to produce efficient machine-made goods with a beauty peculiar to themselves. As a result of propaganda on the part of individuals, the B.B.C., and the Design and Industries Association, well-designed goods are once again being demanded. Manufacturers are beginning to employ designers to study and exploit their materials and methods of production so that the goods they market are beautiful as well as efficient. In the home the interest in the design of everyday things is extending from the equipment and furnishing to the actual structure itself. In consequence the architect is being asked to produce houses and flats which give the owners maximum scope for present-day living and which have their own intrinsic beauty.

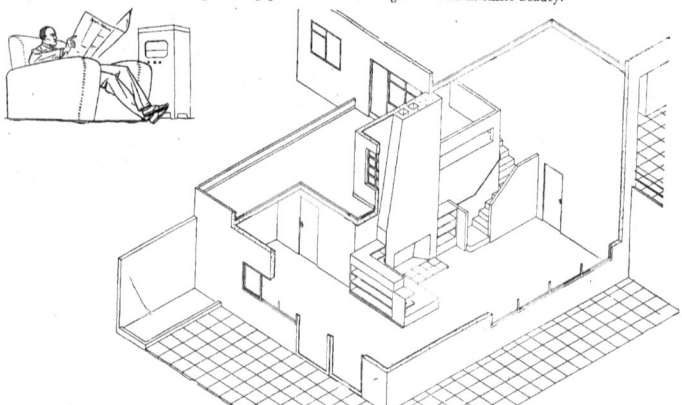

Contemporary social and economic conditions give the modern flat, house, and week-end cottage common characteristics. That is, of course, if the owner accepts life today and does not pretend he is living in the past. The comparatively small amount of time spent in the home has made the modern dwelling small in size—it may even be a one-room flat for a bachelor. The desire for a feeling of spaciousness has resulted in the many ground-floor rooms of the nineteenth-century house being thrown into one large living space subdivided by built-in furniture or screens into zones for the different activities. The expense and shortage of domestic labour necessitates labour-saving equipment and easily cleaned surfaces. The demand for fresh air and sunlight is responsible for large windows and the extension of rooms into the open air by means of terraces and balconies. The reluctance to be tied down by cumbersome articles requires the wardrobes, kitchen fittings, and other bulky equipment to be "built-in" as an integral part of the structure. The noise and high speed of everyday existence is responsible for the use of sound-proofing materials, restful lighting, and simple colour schemes and textures. Above all, the frank acceptance of all that this mechanical era can offer and impatience with sentimental reconstructions of past styles produce designs permeated by what, for lack of a better word, is called the "modern" spirit. The drawing above of a house at Hatfield designed by F. R. S. Yorke, shows a typical "open" plan with its large living space with sitting zone round the fire, and dining zone on the left with its own door to the kitchen.

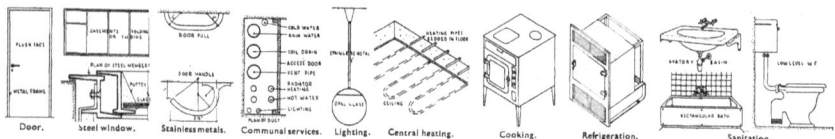

Door. Steel window. Stainless metals. Communal services. Lighting. Central heating. Cooking. Refrigeration. Sanitation.

ARCHITECTURAL CHARACTER: *Modern* (page 46). The plan is "open" with one large living space subdivided into "zones" for the various activities. The rooms for sleeping and bathing are small, and there is a complete absence of thick internal walls, corridors, and other waste space. Free planning, with properly orientated rooms and large windows in any desired position, is made possible by the flat roof and the adoption of contemporary materials such as reinforced concrete and steel. The elevations arise naturally from the plan and rely for their effect on pure form, the textures of the various materials, and the use of clean bright colours. In flats the "cantilever" (page 42) is a feature, as, by means of this, the living-rooms can be extended into the open air in the form of balconies. Windows are steel of the folding, sliding, or casement type, and on the south and west elevations are exceptionally large. Doors are of the flush variety. Internally the rooms are finished in plaster distempered or painted, wood, marble, tile, cork, rubber, glass, and building board. The choice of material depends upon the function of the room and the textures and colours required for the æsthetic effect. The dwelling is fully equipped with central heating, electric lighting, and power, cold water and plumbing services, telephone and wireless, all designed as an integral part of, and contained within, the building. ● BUILDINGS TO SEE. Flats: High Point, Highgate, N. 6, by Tecton; Kensall House, Ladbroke Grove, W. 10, by a *committee of architects*; Lawn Road, Hampstead, N.W. 3, by Wells Coates; Park Court, Crystal Palace, S.E. 26, and Ellington Court, Southgate, N. 14, by the author. Other flat buildings and houses can be found in two books, "The Modern Flat" and "The Modern House in England" (The Architectural Press).

69. *Cottage at Richmond, Yorkshire.* 1940. *Architect : Denis Clarke-Hall.*

70. *Interior, House at Esher.* 1939. *Architects : Patrick Gwynne and Wells Coates.*

71. *Terrace, Stratford-on-Avon.* 1939. *Architect : F. R. S. Yorke.*

72. *House at Highgate.* 1940. *Architects : Tayler and Green.*

73. *Flats at Pullman Court, Streatham.* 1934. *Architect : Frederick Gibberd.*

The modern dwelling is of a variety of types and is built of a variety of materials. The examples shown here are a single-floor detached bungalow, in stone and concrete, 69; a terrace of rural cottages in brick and timber, 71; a three-storey town house in brick and concrete with rendered finish, 72; and a multi-floor block of one- and two-room flats in reinforced concrete.

20TH CENTURY • 1935-   MODERN

1935 George V's Jubilee. -36 Edward VIII. George VI. ● The world is now undergoing a state of change and is, in consequence, suffering from growing pains. The scientist and inventor have banished the fear of scarcity; there is more than enough food for the whole of the population; mass production has provided manufactured goods for all; aviation and wireless telegraphy have abolished distance and broken down national barriers. And yet throughout the world there is poverty amidst plenty, local tribal worship and petty superstitions. Those very things that have made possible a brotherhood of man are used to estrange one people from another. Wireless and the press are used for insidious propaganda; the aeroplane as an instrument of warfare; and the food and raw materials of the world as elements for political bargaining, with the result that there is suspicion, mistrust, large scale rearmament, and fear of war. At home the financial crisis of 1931 made us aware of the extreme delicacy of our economical and political organizations, and, in consequence, steps towards national planning are being taken in the formation of chartered corporations, public utility companies, and agricultural boards. Fine systems of education, health service, sanitation, broadcasting, fire fighting, postal and telephone service, have already been built up; and the attention of the Government is being directed to the problems of housing, malnutrition and physical fitness. The electric grid system and motor transport have given a new mobility to industry—factories are no longer tied down to canals, railways, and coal mines. Gas and electricity have made possible the clean town, the science of acoustics the silent one, and modern architecture the efficient and beautiful one. A national plan is required to coordinate all these and the other activities and services that are now at our disposal. Only by research into the needs of the community and a concrete plan to direct future development can such problems as overcrowding in cities, traffic confusion, and agricultural stagnation be solved. If this country is to be made a fit place for Englishmen to live in, a concentrated effort at planning and reconstruction must be made; if it is to be made once more a beautiful place to live in, then the architect must be asked to take his part.

The invention of plywood, in which thin layers of wood are cemented together so that the grain pulls in opposite directions and does not, therefore, warp, makes possible large flush wood surfaces. The flush door or wall finish now supersedes the old panelled variety. Below is shown a few of the many contemporary building materials.

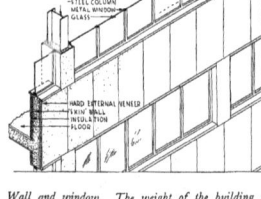

Wall and window. The weight of the building is carried on a rigid framework. Owing to the development of insulating materials the wall may now be a thin skin to keep out the weather. Light steel sections for windows allow thin members with the opening portions to be arranged as casements, to slide or to fold.

New insulating and waterproofing materials, such as cork, fibre board and bituminous felts, make possible the flat roof. Apart from a saving in material, the flat roof allows much greater freedom in planning, as a pitched roof, if it is to be reasonably constructed, must be over simple rectangular shapes:

MODERN

There is now a growing conviction that architecture should not be restricted by shaping it in some past style, which, as we have seen, arises out of quite different social conditions and methods of building ; and that the new materials and methods of construction which science has given us, if honestly used, are capable of having an architectural expression of their own. Furthermore, the social changes that have taken place require many new architectural forms which are incapable of being forced into those to which we are accustomed. The result of this is that a new architectural development is taking place which attempts to unite science and art. For the sake of a better word it is called " Modern." The struggle for an honest architectural expression can be traced back to the beginning of the century, but it is not until the year 1936 that any real amount of work is executed.

BUILDING ACTIVITY. Buildings of all types erected by individuals who are conscious that contemporary needs require a contemporary architecture. ● **ARCHITECTURAL CHARACTER**: *Modern.* Particular characteristics are: open planning (page 44) ; walls being no longer weight carrying can be replaced by thin screens and partitions, allowing large open spaces where desired. The Frame, 75: in steel or reinforced concrete structures the frame is expressed as such and not disguised. The Skin Wall, 74: as the external wall is solely to keep out the weather, it is treated as a thin skin and not made to look as if it held the building up. The Flat Roof: new insulating and waterproofing materials make the flat roof in many cases more economical and efficient than the pitched variety. The Cantilever, 69: reinforced concrete allows projections to be cantilevered straight out from a wall without supporting columns or brackets. Absence of external ornament, 76: rustication or bands of ornament tend to confuse the dynamic quality of the skin wall stretched over a frame. Light and Air, 70: large windows admit a maximum of sunlight, radiators correcting the heat losses. Complete Services: plumbing, heating, and other service pipes are contained in ducts as an integral part of the building rather than draped over the walls. Colour and Texture: use of clean bright colours and contrasting textures instead of applied decorations to emphasize the form of the building, 75. Traditional as well as new materials are made use of. **BUILDINGS TO SEE.** Gilbey's, Camden Town, by Serge Chermayeff. London Gliding Club, Dunstable, by Christopher Nicholson. Buildings at London and Whipsnade Zoos, by Tecton. Nurses' Home, Macclesfield General Infirmary, by the Author. Peter Jones, Sloane Square, London, by W. Crabtree in association with Slater and Moberly. Pioneer Health Centre, Peckham, London, by Sir E. Owen Williams. Piccadilly Underground railway stations. Showrooms for Central London Electricity, by E. Maxwell Fry. Simpson's, Piccadilly, London, by Joseph Emberton.

74. Boots' Factory, Nottingham. 1932. Architect : Sir Owen Williams.

75. Colliery, Wallsend. 1935. Architect : R. A. Cordingley.

76. Methodist Mission, Colliers Wood, London. 1938. Architect : E. D. Mills.

77. Bexhill Pavilion. 1935. Architects : Mendelsohn and Chermayeff.

78. Impington Village College. Architects : Walter Gropius and E. Maxwell Fry.

79. Foreshore Development, Folkestone. 1937. Architect : D. Pleydell-Bouverie.

The revivals of past styles are abandoned for a new architecture which exploits traditional and new building materials for contemporary needs. Whether the buildings are of glass and concrete, 74, brick, 76, 78, steel and cement rendering, 77, brick and concrete, 79, or glass faced, 80, they have a consistent architectural character just as Gothic had in the fourteenth century (p. 15), or Georgian in the eighteenth century (p. 31).

80. Finsbury Health Centre. 1938. Architects : Tecton.

INDEX

	Page
Adam Brothers	30, 31
Agriculture	16, 22, 28
Aldeburgh, Moot Hall	19
Aqueduct, Roman	7
Arch: four-centred	16
Norman	8, 9
pointed	10, 12
Arch of Titus, Rome	7
Architect engineers	38
Architrave	6, 22
Balcony	34, 35, 42, 45
Barlow	38, 39
Barnfield Crescent, Exeter	33
Barnsley, G.	43
Basilica, early Christian	6
Bath, heated by gas	36
Bayeux tapestry	8
Bessemer	38
Bexhill Pavilion	47
Bishop Hooper's Lodgings, Gloucester	10
Blenheim Palace, Oxfordshire	29
Blomfield, Sir R.	41
Boots' Factory, Nottingham	47
Boss	14
Brick, the standard	18
Bridges: Craigellachie	39
Cringleford	19
Crumlin Viaduct	38
Hungerford	38
Brixton, house at	35
Brocklesby Park, Lincs	41
Brunel	38
Bush House, London	43
Buttresses	8, 10, 12
Cannon, fifteenth-century	16
Carlton House Terrace	34, 35
Casement	24, 44
Castles: Dover	9
Norman	8
Stokesay	11
(See also *Buildings to See*, page 8)	
Cathedral, the	12
Cathedrals: Durham	8, 9
Exeter	15
Hereford	9
Norwich	8
St. Paul's	26, 27
Lincoln	10, 13
Westminster Abbey	12
York Minster	11
(See also *Buildings to See*, pages 8, 10, 14, 16)	
Chimneys at Hampton Court	19
Churches: City, the	26
Early Christian	6
Romanesque	6
St. Bride's, Fleet Street	27
St. Stephen's Walbrook	26
Sutton, Cambridgeshire	15
typical plan	6, 10
Classic architecture	22, 23, 26-35
Colliery, Wallsend	47
Colosseum, Rome	7
Column and lintel construction	6
Columns	6, 7, 22, 40
Communications: aeroplane	40, 46
canals	34
coach	26
cycling	40
horse bus	34
motor car	42
railway	38
Compton Wynyates, gateway	18
Concrete	40
Cordingley, R.A.	47
Cornice	6, 22
Cottage, the	24
Cottage, fourteenth-century	14
Cottage at Cherhill, Wiltshire	25
Cottage at Richmond, Yorkshire	45
Cottage, Kent, boarded	28
"Cruciform" plan, the	12
Crystal Palace, roof of the	38, 39
Cupola	26
"Decorated" architecture	14
Details (decoration, ornament, etc.): Adam	30
Decorated	14
Early English	10

	Page
Details (decoration, ornament, etc.): eighteenth-century	32
Elizabethan	20
Jazz	42
Norman	8
Perpendicular	16
Regency	34
Tudor	18
Victorian	36
Don's House, an Oxford	37
Doors: cottage, boarded	24
eighteenth-century	28, 32
medieval, boarded	16
twentieth-century, flush	44, 46
Dormer windows	24, 28
Dressing (in stone)	28
Early Christian architecture	6
Early English architecture	10
Early Georgian architecture	28
Edwardian architecture	40
Eighteenth century	28-33
Elizabethan architecture	20
Eltham Hall, Kent	17
Fan vaulting	16, 17
Feudal system, the	8
Fifteenth century	16, 17
Finsbury Health Centre	47
Flats: Ealing	43
Pullman Court, Streatham	45
St. John's Wood	43
Flying buttresses	12
Folkestone, foreshore development at	42
Four-centred arch, the	16
Fourteenth century	14, 15
Frieze	6, 18
Fry, E. Maxwell	47
Gable	29
Gatehouse, Stokesay Castle	21
Gateway, Compton Wynyates	18
George V, architecture of	42, 43
George VI, architecture of	46
Georgian architecture	28-33
Georgian house, the	32
Gibberd, Frederick	45
Gothic architecture	10-17
Gray and Evans	43
Great Exhibition, the	36
Greek architecture	6
Greenwich Hospital	26
Gropius, Walter	47
Gwynne, Patrick, and Wells Coates	45
Hall, Denis Clarke-	45
Hall, E. T. and S.	43
Hammer-beam roof	16, 17
Hampton Court Palace, chimneys at	19
Hansom, J. A.	37
Hare, H. T.	41
Hatfield, house at	44, 47
Heating	14, 20, 24, 32, 40, 44
Helmle and Corbett	43
Heraldry	14, 15, 18
Hipped roofs	22
Holkham Hall, Norfolk, plan of	28
Houses: Brixton	35
Esher	45
Georgian	32
Highgate	45
Industrial North	35
Malvern	41
medieval	44
modern	44
Queen Anne's Gate	29
Regency	34, 35
seventeenth-century	22
sixteenth-century	20
Victorian	36
Housing schemes: Essex	43
Welwyn, Herts	43
Impington Village College	47
Inigo Jones	22, 23
Insurance Building, Strand	41
Interior, late Victorian	37
Interior, 99, Great Russell St., London	32
Iron, wrought	36, 38
Iron, cast-	42
Jazz	42
Keep, a Norman	8
Kent, William	28

	Page
Kingpost	16
King's College Chapel, Cambridge	17
Kirby Hall, Northants	21
Kitchener, the patent	34
Knight, serf and clerk	10
Knole Park, Sevenoaks	21
Landscape gardening, eighteenth-century	30
Late Georgian architecture	30
Leeds Post Office	37
Leighs Priory, Essex	19
Liberty's, London	43
Liernes	14
Lincoln Cathedral	13
Lloyd's Coffee House	28
Magdalen College, Oxford, the Tower	17
Manors	8
Mass production	42
Medieval agriculture	16
Medieval door, the	16
Medieval house, plan of the	14
Mendelsohn and Chermayeff	47
Methodist Mission, Colliers Wood, London	47
Mills, E. D.	47
Modern dwelling, the	44
Modernistic architecture	42
Montacute House, Somerset, plan of	20
Moot Hall, Aldeburgh	19
Morden College, Blackheath	27
Mullions	10, 18, 22
Nash, John	34, 35
Nineteenth century	34-39
Norman architecture	8
Norman castle keep, a	8
Norman village, sketch of	8
Norwich Union Insurance Building	41
Offices, Liverpool	37
"Ogee" (reversed curve)	14
Orangery, Kensington	26
"Orchards," Godalming, the	41
Orders, the	6
"Palladian" architecture	22
Panelling	18, 26, 32, 46
Pantheon, the	6
Parapet	10, 22
Parish church plan, typical	16
Parthenon, the	6, 7
Paxton	39
Penshurst Place, Kent	15
Perpendicular architecture	16, 17
Piccadilly Circus in 1901	40
Piers	8, 10, 12
Pilasters	20, 21
Pinnacles	10, 12
Plans: Holkham Hall, Norfolk	28
house of 1830	34
house of 1870	36
medieval house	14
Montacute House, Somerset	20
Norman village	8
Norwich Cathedral	8
Regent's Park	34
St. Stephen's Walbrook	26
typical parish church	16
Westminster Abbey	12
Wren's plan of London	26
Pleydell-Bouverie, D.	47
Pont du Gard, Nimes	7
Post Office, Leeds	37
Prince Regent, the	34
Prudential Building, Holborn, the	37
Pullman Court, Streatham, flats at	45
Queen Elizabeth visiting Lord Hunsdon	20
Queen's House, Greenwich	22, 23
Regal Theatre, Sunderland	43
Regency architecture	34, 35
Regent's Park, plan of	34
Revivals	36, 37, 40-43
Ribs, vaulting	12, 14
Richmond, cottage at	45
Roman architecture	6
Romanesque architecture	6

	Page
Roofs: flat	46
hammer-beam	16, 17
hipped	22
iron and glass	38, 39
ridge and furrow	38
tie-beam	16
trussed rafter	16
Royal Society, the	26
Rusticated base	22
St. Bride's, Fleet Street	27
St. James's Park in 1790	30
St. Pancras Station	39
St. Paul's Cathedral	26, 27
St. Philip's, Birmingham	29
St. Stephen's Walbrook, plan of	26
Salisbury Cathedral	10
Sanitation	10, 24, 36, 44
Seventeenth century	22, 23, 26, 27
Shaw, N.	37
Sheep farming	14
Ships: eighteenth century	30
Elizabethan	20
nineteenth century	38
seventeenth century	22
Sixteenth century	18-21
Skipper, G. J. and F. W.	41
Solar, Knole Park, Sevenoaks, the	21
"Sovereign of the Seas," the	22
Speculative suburban dwellings	43
Steel construction	36, 38, 40
Stokesay Castle	11, 21
Stratford-on-Avon, terrace at	45
Sutton Church, Cambridgeshire	15
Tanner, H.	37
Tayler and Green	45
Tecton	47
Telford	38, 39
Thirteenth century	10, 11
Thorpe Hall, Peterborough	23
Toms and Partners	43
"Tooth and Gap"	42
Town Hall, Birmingham	37
Transitional buildings, twentieth century	42
Transomes	18, 22
Transport (see Communications)	
Trussed rafter	16
Tudor architecture	18, 19
Twelfth century	8, 9
Twentieth century	40-47
Urban development: eighteenth century	31, 32
nineteenth century	37
twentieth century	42, 43
Vanbrugh	28, 29
Vaulting, decorated	14, 15
fan	16, 17
Norman system of	8
ribs	12, 14
Victorian architecture	36, 37
Victorian interior, late	37
Voysey, C. F. A.	41
Wall and Window: Classic	22
Early English	10
eighteenth century	28
modern	46
Norman	8
Tudor	18
Watt, James	30
Weather clock, Wren's model of	26
Webb, John	22, 23
Westminster Abbey	12
Williams, Sir Owen	47
Wimperis, Simpson and Guthrie	43
Windmills	16, 22
Windows: dormer	24, 28
iron casement	24
Perpendicular	12
steel	44
York Minster	11, 15
(See also under Wall and Window)	
Wingless Victory, Temple of	7
Wren, Sir Christopher	26, 27
Wright, Frank	40
York Minster	11, 15
Yorke, F. R. S.	44, 45

www.ingramcontent.com/pod-product-compliance
Ingram Content Group UK Ltd.
Pitfield, Milton Keynes, MK11 3LW, UK
UKHW041948230426
12048UKWH00008B/204